FRENCH
KEY WORDS

is a learning aid benefiting from computer analysis of 500,000 words. It consists of a list of the commonest two thousand key words in French, with their meanings in English, arranged in decreasing order of frequency. The list is divided into a hundred units of twenty key words each, from which many more words can be derived. For masculine adjectives, feminine endings are given if irregular. For singular nouns, plurals are given if irregular. All the commonest irregular verbs are cited fully in the present indicative, with meanings, and the four regular conjugations are listed separately.

Xavier-Yves Escande has made sure that pupils in the first year of secondary school, or adult beginners, will be introduced to all the most frequently-occurring words in French within the first year of study. An English index allows the user to trace each word in the lists, and a French index traces each word in the lists and indicates by its position in the book the relative frequency of that word. Some readers may not have realised that the commonest hundred words in French include only four nouns: can you guess what they might be? The answer is given in the introduction to Xavier-Yves Escande's *French Key Words*

FRENCH KEY WORDS

the basic 2,000-word vocabulary
arranged by frequency in a
hundred units

with comprehensive French and
English indexes

XAVIER-YVES ESCANDE

The Oleander Press

The Oleander Press
17 Stansgate Avenue
Cambridge CB2 2QZ
England

The Oleander Press
210 Fifth Avenue
N.Y. 10010
U.S.A.

British Library Cataloguing in Publication Data

Escande, Xavier-Yves
  French key words.—(Oleander language and
  literature; v.14)
  1. French language—Dictionaries—English
  2. English language—Dictionaries—French
  I. Title
  443'.21   PC2640

  ISBN 0-906672-23-6
  ISBN 0-906672-24-4 Pbk

Designed by Geoff Green

Printed and bound in Great Britain at
The Camelot Press Ltd, Southampton

CONTENTS

Introduction

French Key Words has been designed as an efficient, logical, and practical computer-based word-list for anglophone learners of French in their first year. The basic two thousand 'key' words are so called because by learning these one unlocks the door to several thousand more words: plurals from singulars, feminines from masculines, and parts of the present tense from an infinitive.

The purpose of this technique is to stimulate confidence in the learning of French by teaching the commonest words first, and leaving the less common till later. *French Key Words* is intended to be used with a conventional grammar and a conventional dictionary, but a massive dictionary has been found in practice to unnerve the beginner, while most available readers introduce too early words or ideas which may be arbitrary or advanced. At this sensitive phase, where interest in learning French can be so easily encouraged or discouraged, it is suggested that the student should be asked to learn words in a hundred units of about twenty 'key' words, thus mastering two thousand such words by the end of the first year. Only then will he or she be ready to absorb arbitrary words of low occurrence. Computer-based methods are by now fully familiar in mathematics and the sciences, but statistical sampling has hitherto been rarely practised in language learning, probably because of the difficulty of establishing a sufficiently large sample to make the frequency list reliable. *French Key Words* is an ideal revision aid for first-year examinations, because you know you *must* know all these words.

The Units

Each of the hundred units is self-contained, Unit 1 including the twenty commonest key words, Unit 2 the next commonest and so on. The key word is following by an indication of its part of speech: *adj.*, adjective; *adv.*, adverb; *conj.*, conjunction; *f.n.*, feminine noun; *m.n.*, masculine noun; *prep.*, preposition; *pron.*, pronoun. Verbs are not so shown, because they are represented by the infinitive, which is in every case translated beginning with 'to'.

Masculine nouns and adjectives form their feminine by adding *e* unless otherwise shown. So masculine *vert* becomes feminine *verte*.

Singular nouns and adjectives form their plural by adding *s* unless otherwise shown. So singular *vert* becomes plural *verts*, and singular *verte* becomes plural *vertes*. *Le livre vert* in the plural becomes *les livres verts* and *la maison verte* becomes *les maisons vertes*.

Regular verbs are conjugated in the present tense in model form in a separate table. The commonest irregular verbs are conjugated in the present tense (of the active voice, indicative mood), wherever their infinitive occurs in the order of frequency. Though verbs appear only under their infinitive form, their position in the units is judged from the total occurrence of all their parts. Occasionally a phrase connected with a word, usually a verb, has been inserted where the phrase is particularly common or could not be constructed without special knowledge.

Homographs are shown as one word if multiple meanings share one part of speech (*boîte*, box and night-club), but as two or more words if they do not: mort, *f.n.*, meaning 'death' in Unit 18 but mort, *adj.* meaning 'a (masculine) dead person' in Unit 54.

Many French words may be translated by a number of English equivalents. It would be counter-productive, in a work designed to stimulate the interest rather than clog the memory, to list all such equivalents, so only the most common have been cited. When consulting the indexes, therefore, the reader should try to think of synonyms or near-synonyms if a given word appears not to be included.

The Indexes

The two indexes permit the reader to use *French Key Words* as a basic dictionary, but once again let it be stressed that the best available dictionary should be purchased if it is intended to continue with French past the elementary stage. Another fascinating use of the indexes is to discover how frequent — and consequently how relatively useful — each French word happens to be. Of course, the frequency level applies only to the *French* words: nothing is implied at any point about the relative frequency of their English equivalents. Even the most casual learner may be curious to learn that among the hundred most frequent words in French only four are nouns: if you care to guess which they are, the answer appears at the end of this Introduction.

Apart from the indefinite and definite articles (*un, une; le, la*), if one counts the indefinite article also as a numeral, then only one other numeral (*deux*) occurs among the commonest hundred. Eleven are prepositions, six conjunctions, 22 pronouns, 19 adverbs, 14 adjectives, and twenty verbs, including the auxiliaries *aller, avoir, être,* and *faire.*

The first ten words are so common that they account for 30.52% of total occurrences, if the commonest 5000 words are taken as 100%; the first hundred account for 62.66% of all occurrences; the first thousand for 85.58%.

The Sources

The word-list has been based on a wide variety of sources, but primarily on Alphonse Juilland and others' *Frequency Dictionary of French Words* (1970), by kind permission of the publishers Mouton, The Hague. Adjustments in the order of frequency have been necessary to take into consideration the somewhat different results obtained by earlier writers. All these writers have been motivated by, as Juilland puts it, "the importance of establishing a more standardized approach to vocabulary, in order to overcome the nearly chaotic inconsistency of teaching materials chosen largely on subjective grounds".

V. A. C. Henmon's *French Word Book* (1924) contained 3,905 key words from a sample of 400,000 running words deriving from a wide variety of sources. C. F. Ward's *Minimum French Vocabulary Test Book* (1926) drew not on French texts, but on word counts of English, a method known from later research on comparative word counts to be unreliable. His claim to have sampled more than ten million words may, therefore, be regarded as not strictly relevant. Ward's *Minimum* contained 2,000 words, five times as many as F. M. Baker's *Vocabulary for First Year French Students* (1928). Baker's subjective criteria for inclusion included classroom terminology, foods, and days of the week, even if they did occur as frequently as other words. Though Baker used Henmon's pioneering work in her own compilation, it is notable that only 68.3% of her 400 words also occur in Henmon.

G. Vander Beke's *French Word Book* (1929) was undertaken to improve on Henmon, increasing the sample to more than 1.14 million words, and the final list to 6,136 words. *A Basic French Vocabulary* (1934) was compiled by a committee chaired by J.B. Tharp and published in *Modern Language Journal* (Vol. XVIII, pp. 238 – 274). Each of the four committee-members relied on a different method for compiling his own preliminary list, which was then compared with the others. Thus, of the 2,752 entries, 2,395 comprised the primary list which were admitted unanimously; the remaining 357 comprised the secondary list, admitted only by a majority vote.

J.D. Haygood's *Le Vocabulaire fondamental du français* (1937) studied G. Vander Beke's *French Word Book*, and came to the conclusion that, since about 90% of the words in his five-book sample were included within the first 2,069 words in Vander Beke, those words constituted a sufficient minimum list for the early years of French.

M. West and O. Bond's *A Grouped Frequency French Word List* (1939), also based on Vander Beke, sought to help teachers by grouping together words of a common derivation roughly on the Roget's *Thesaurus* principle, with a total of 2,019 entries, that is 78% of Vander Beke's total. Other compilations based largely on Vander Beke include B. Schlyter's *Centrala Ordförradet i Franskan* (1951) and Verlée's *Basis-Woordenboek voor de Franse Taal* (1954).

The next independent enterprise in this field was *L'Elaboration du français élémentaire* (1956) and its successor *Le Français fondamental* (1959). Sponsored by the Ministère de l'Education Nationale, the *Français fondamental* project aimed to establish a basic French to be taught quickly to foreigners so that they could cope with situations arising in daily life. Thus the compilers, chaired by G. Gougenheim, relied on 163 taped conversations of varying length, and derived from this sample 312,000 words which were reduced to 1,063 words with a frequency of 20 + and 6,872 less common words are also tabulated.

R.L. Politzer's *Programmed Dictionary for Masterpieces of French Literature* (1966) reverts for a model to Vander Beke, but takes into account the *Français élémentaire* and *Français fondamental* lists, to a total of 6,500 words, but this is not geared to the elementary learner, and omits most functional words and many obvious cognates.

The most serious undertaking of all, from the viewpoint of statistical reliability, has been that of Juilland and others, with their policy of equalizing subsamples. Thus, Vander Beke used units of 10,000 words each as follows: 33 units (38.82%) from fiction, 13 units (15.3%) from drama, 9 units (10.59%) from science, religion and philosophy, 16 units (18.82%) from biography, history and criticism, and 14 units (16.47%) from newspapers and journals. Juilland rightly points out that weighting cannot be justified without reference to a specific purpose, which a first-year student does not yet possess, and equalizes subsamples by deriving a sample of 500,000 words from five equal genres: drama, fiction, essays, scientific and technical works, and newspapers and magazines.

The frequency ratings of Juilland have been followed quite closely, except that where his ratings differ significantly from those of his rivals, a compromise has been reached, making the following lists probably even more accurate over the whole range of French than any preceding work. Words which have been eliminated by most previous writers as unsuitable are those common only before 1920, including archaicisms; words which have just entered the language in the last two or three decades, including neologisms; and slang, dialect or regional words which form part of the undergrowth of language, rarely surfacing in newspapers, journals, or books.

December 1983   *Xavier-Yves Escande*

N.B. The four nouns occurring in the commonest hundred words are *monsieur* and *homme* (Unit 4) and *jour* and *temps* (Unit 5).

Regular Verbs in
the Present Tense

First Conjugation

je parle   I speak
tu parles   you (*s.*) speak
il, elle parle   he, she speaks

Parler, to speak

nous parlons   we speak
vous parlez   you (*pl.*) speak
ils, elles parlent   they speak

Second Conjugation

je finis   I finish
tu finis   you (*s.*) finish
il, elle finit   he, she finishes

Finir, to finish

nous finissons   we finish
vous finissez   you (*pl.* speak)
ils, elles finissent   they speak

Third Conjugation

je reçois   I receive
tu reçois   you (*s.*) receive
il, elle reçoit   he, she receives

Recevoir, to receive

nous recevons   we receive
vous recevez   you (*pl.*) receive
ils, elles reçoivent   they receive

Fourth Conjugation

je rends   I give up
tu rends   you (*s.*) give up
il, elle rend   he, she gives up

Rendre, to give up, render

nous rendons   we give up
vous rendez   you (*pl.*) give up
ils, elles rendent   they give up

Unit 1

le (*m.*), la (*f.*),
    l' before vowel or silent
    'h', (*pl.* les) *pron.* — the

un (*m.*), une (*f.*) *pron.* — a, an

de *prep.* — of, from

être — to be, being

    je suis I am   nous sommes we are
    tu es you (*s.*) are   vous êtes you (*pl.*) are
    il, elle est he, she, it is   ils, elles sont they are

et *conj.* — and

à *prep.* — to, at

il (*pl.* ils) *pron.* — he, it (*m.*), they (*m.*)

elle (*pl.* elles) *pron.* — she, it (*f.*), they (*f.*)

ne *adv.* — not

que *pron.* — that, which, whom

du (*m.*), de la (*f.*)
    (*pl.* des) *prep., pron.* — of the, from the

avoir — to have

    j'ai I have   nous avons we have
    tu as you (*s.*) have   vous avez you (*pl.*) have
    il, elle a he, she has   ils, elles ont they have

ce (*m.*), cette (*f.*)
    (*pl.* ces) *adj.* — this, these

Unit 2

qui *pron.* — that, which, who

se, s' before vowel or silent 'h' *pron.* — oneself, himself, herself, itself, themselves

en *prep.* — in, into

dans *prep.* — in, into (inside)

au (*m.*), à la (*f.*) or à l' before vowel or silent 'h' (*pl.* aux) *prep., pron.* — to the, at the

ce, c' before vowel or silent 'h' *pron.* — it, that

pas *adv.* — not

son (*m.*), sa (*f.*) (*pl.* ses) *adj.* — one's, his, her, its

pour *prep.* — for

plus *adv.* — more

on *pron.* — one (impersonal)

par *prep.* — by

sur *prep.* — on, upon

mais *adv.* — but

tout (*m.*), toute (*f.*) (*pl.* tous, toutes) *adj.* — all, every

Unit 3

pouvoir — to be able

    je peux, puis   I can, am able   nous pouvons   we can
    tu peux   you (*s.*) can   vous pouvez   you (*pl.*) can
    il, elle peut   he, she can   ils, elles peuvent   they can

avec *prep.* — with

le (*m.*), la (*f.*) — him, her, it, them
    (*pl.* les)   *pron.*   (to replace a noun)

faire — to make, do

    je fais   I make   nous faisons   we make
    tu fais   you (*s.*) make   vous faites   you (*pl.*) make
    il, elle fait   he, she makes   ils, elles font   they make

comme *adv.* — as, like

me *pron.* — me

dire — to say

    je dis   I say   nous disons   we say
    tu dis   you (*s.*) say   vous dites   you (*pl.*) say
    il, elle dit   he, she says   ils, elles disent   they say

y *adv., pron.* — here, there (used only in compounds: J'y suis, j'y reste! Here I am and here I stay; otherwise see ici, là)

en *adv., pron.* — from there, on that account, of it, of them, some (j'en ai, I have some; je n'en ai pas, I haven't any of them)

bien *adv.* — well

lui (*pl.* eux) *pron.* — him, them

ou *conj.* — or

si *conj.* — if

leur *adj.* — their

où *adv.* — where

mon (*m.*), ma (*f.*) — my
    (*pl.* mes)   *pron.*

Unit 4

voir — to see

    je vois — I see   nous voyons — we see
    tu vois — you (s.) see   vous voyez — you (pl.) see
    il, elle voit — he, she sees   ils, elles voient — they see

sans *prep.* — without

même *adj.* — same

notre *adj.* — our

    (*pl.* nos)

encore *adv.* — still, yet

grand *adj.* — tall, big, large, great

savoir — to know

    je sais — I know   nous savons — we know
    tu sais — you know   nous savez — you know
    il, elle saît — he, she knows   ils, elles savent — they know

quelque *adj., adv.* — some, any

peu *adv.* — little, few

venir — to come

    je viens — I come   nous venons — we come
    tu viens — you come   vous venez — you come
    il, elle vient — he, she comes   ils, elles viennent — they come

aussi *adv.* — as, so, also, too

donner — to give

très *adv.* — very

devoir — to have to, owe

    je dois — I must   nous devons — we must
    tu dois — you must   vous devez — you must
    il, elle doit — he, she must   ils, elles doivent — they must

monsieur *m.n.* — Mr, sir, gentleman

    (*pl.* messieurs)

falloir — to be necessary

    il faut   it is necessary

homme *m.n.* — man, husband

tout *adv.* — quite, entirely

Unit 5

petit *adj.*	small, short
jour *m.n.*	day, daylight
autre *adj.*	other
dont *pron.*	from ⎫ by ⎬ whom, which with ⎭
rien *pron.*	nothing, anything
vouloir	to want, wish

je veux		nous voulons	
tu veux		vous voulez	
il, elle veut		ils, elles veulent	

trouver	to find
moins *adv.*	less
cela, ça	that (fact, thing) e.g. Cela coûte mille francs That (thing) costs 1,000 francs
là *adv.*	there (of a place)
même *adv.*	even
non *adv.*	no, not
croire	to believe, think

je crois		nous croyons	
tu crois		vous croyez	
il, elle croit		ils, elles croient	

quand *conj.*	when
prendre	to take

je prends		nous prenons	
tu prends		vous prenez	
il, elle prend		ils, elles prennent	

si *adv.*	so, so much
premier (*m.*), première (*f.*) *adj.*	first
temps *m.n.*	time, weather
toujours *adv.*	always, ever

Unit 6

celui (*m.*), celle (*f.*) (*pl.*) ceux, celles *pron.*	he, she, they, that, those
heure *f.n.*	hour, time
tout *pron.*	all, everything
bon (*m.*), bonne (*f.*) *adj.*	good, fine, nice
aller	to go

je vais	nous allons
tu vas	vous allez
il, elle va	ils, elles vont

moi *pron.*	I (stressed), me
seul *adj.*	only, alone, single
alors *adv.*	at that time, then
fois *f.n.*	time (quatre fois, four times)
mettre	to place, put

je mets	nous mettons
tu mets	vous mettez
il, elle met	ils, elles mettent

vie *f.n.*	life
sous *prep.*	below, under
après *prep.*	after
chose *f.n.*	thing
jamais *adv.*	never, ever
parler	to speak
entre *prep.*	between

Unit 7

donc *conj.*	so, therefore
tenir	to hold
je tiens	nous tenons
tu tiens	vous tenez
il, elle tient	ils, elles tiennent
beau (bel before vowel or silent 'h') (*m.*), belle (*f.*), (*pl.* beaux, belles) *adj.*	beautiful, handsome, fine
autre *pron.*	other
jusque (jusqu' before vowel or silent 'h') *prep.*	until, up to
laisser	to let, leave
quel (*m.*), quelle (*f.*) *adj.*	what, which
trop *adv.*	too, too much, too many
ici *adv.*	here
chez *prep.*	at, with
depuis *prep.*	since, for
rester	to remain
ainsi *adv.*	so, thus, like this
femme *f.n.*	woman, wife
déjà *adv.*	already, before
certain *adj.*	some, sure, certain
passer	to pass, cross

Unit 8

an *m.n.*	year
demander	to ask
moment *m.n.*	moment
assez *adv.*	enough, sufficiently
connaître	to know (be acquainted with)

    je connais   nous connaissons
    tu connais   vous connaissez
    il, elle connaît   ils, elles connaissent

ni *conj.*	neither, nor
beaucoup *adv.*	much, a great deal
sembler	seem, appear

nouveau (nouvel before vowel
    or silent 'h') (*m.*),
    nouvelle (*f.*),
    (*pl.* nouveaux, nouvelles)
	new

monde *m.n.*	world
tel (*m.*), telle (*f.*) (*pl.* telles) *adj.*	such
dernier (*m.*), dernière (*f.*) *adj.*	last, latest
penser	to think
oeil *m.n.* (*pl.* yeux)	eye
chaque *adj.*	each, every
car *conj.*	because, for
paraître	to seem, appear

    je parais   nous paraissons
    tu parais   vous paraissez
    il, elle paraît   ils, elles paraissent

Unit 9

jeune *adj.*	young
devenir	to become (conjugated like venir)
votre (*s.*)	your
(*pl.* vos)	
fait *m.n.*	act, occurrence
arriver	to arrive, come
point *m.n.*	point, stitch
seulement *adv.*	only, merely
vers *prep.*	towards, about
guerre *f.n.*	war, warfare
comprendre	to understand, include
enfin *adv.*	at last, in short
peut-être *adv.*	perhaps, possibly
vivre	to live

je vis		nous vivons	
tu vis		vous vivez	
il, elle vit		ils vivent	

tant *adv.*	so much
idée *f.n.*	idea
chercher	to seek, look for
enfant *m. & f.n.*	child, boy, girl
aucun *pron.*	any(one), no(one)
parce que *conj.*	because

Unit 10

lui (*s.*), leur (*pl.*) *pron.*	to him, to them
pendant *prep.*	during
aujourd'hui *adv.*	today
contre *prep.*	against
maintenant *adv.*	now
mot *m.n.*	word
devant *prep.*	before, in front of
travail *m.n.*	work, labour
permettre	to permit (conjugated like mettre)
maison *f.n.*	house
année *f.n.*	year
vieux, vieil (*m.*), vieille (*f.*) *adj.*	old
avant *prep.*	before
revenir	to return (conjugated like venir)
puis *adv.*	then, next, besides
mieux *adv.*	better
aimer	to love

Unit 11

question *f.n.*	question
près *adv.*	near
coup *m.n.*	knock, blow
part *f.n.*	share, part
souvent *adv.*	often
vrai *adj.*	true
force *f.n.*	strength, force
presque, presqu' before vowel or silent 'h' *adv.*	nearly (with negative, hardly)
soir *m.n.*	evening, afternoon
porter	to carry, bear
place *f.n.*	place, seat, square
lorsque, lorsqu' before vowel or silent 'h' *adv.*	(at the moment) when
nom *m.n.*	name
doute *m.n.*	doubt
lieu *m.n.*	place
madame *f.n.*	Mrs, lady
montrer	to show
pays *m.n.*	country, district
côté *m.n.*	side
agir	to act, behave

Unit 12

loin *adv.*	far
nuit *f.n.*	night
appeler, s'appeler	to call, to be called
mois *m.n.*	month
sentir	to feel, smell
ami *m.n.*	friend
cas *m.n.*	case
façon *f.n.*	manner, way
abord *m.n.*, d'abord *adv.*	access, at first
quoi *pron.*	what
attendre	to wait for, await
terre *f.n.*	world, earth
recevoir	to receive
main *f.n.*	hand
commencer	to begin
matin *m.n.*	morning
ville *f.n.*	town
suivre	to follow
tête *f.n.*	head

Unit 13

comment *adv.*	how
entendre	to mean, intend
eau *f.n.*	water
(*pl.* eaux)	
effet *m.n.*	result, effect
regarder	to look at, regard, consider
partir	to leave, set out, part
amour *m.n.*	love
possible *adj.*	possible
jouer	to play
dès *prep.*	as early as, since
esprit *m.n.*	wit, spirit
affaire *f.n.*	business, affair
entrer	to enter
suite *f.n.*	suite, continuation
français *adj.*	French
gens *m.n.* (*pl.*)	men, women, people
cause *f.n.*	cause, legal suit
servir	to serve
long (*m.*), longue (*f.*) *adj.*	long
cœur *m.n.*	heart

Unit 14

corps *m.n.*	body
rappeler	to recall
dieu *m.n.*	god
longtemps *adv.*	for a long time
besoin *m.n.*	want, need
raison *f.n.*	reason (avoir raison, to be right)
partie *f.n.*	part, party
répondre	respond, answer
état *m.n.*	state, list
mouvement *m.n.*	movement, change
ci *adv.*	(in compounds, e.g. par-ci) here
perdre	to lose
voilà *prep.*	there is, there are
retrouver	to regain, find again
porte *f.n.*	gate, door
sortir	leave, go or get out
compte *m.n.*	account
exemple *m.n.*	example
fin *f.n.*	end, purpose
général *adj.* (*pl.* généraux)	general

Unit 15

rendre	to give back, deliver
valeur *f.n.*	value, worth
fond *m.n.*	back (far side), bottom (of pit, etc.)
surtout *adv.*	above all
simple *adj.*	simple, single, easy
pourquoi *adv.*	why (question or statement)
droit *m.n.*	right, law, fee
oui *adv.*	yes
apporter	bring, provide (conjugated like porter)
père *m.n.*	father
mesure *f.n.*	measure
écrire	to write

j'écris		nous écrivons	
tu écris		vous écrivez	
il, elle écrit		ils, elles écrivent	

art *m.n.*	art
présenter	to present
chambre *f.n.*	room
vue *f.n.*	sight, view
plein *adj.*	full
blanc (*m.*), blanche (*f.*) *adj.* (*pl.* blancs, blanches)	white
fille *f.n.*	girl, daughter
reprendre	to retake, resume, recover (conjugated like prendre)

Unit 16

forme *f.n.*	form, shape
mal *adv.*	badly, ill
offrir	to offer

j'offre	nous offrons
tu offres	vous offrez
il, elle offre	ils, elles offrent

livre *m.n.*	book
pourtant *adv.*	however, nevertheless
pied *m.n.*	foot
puisque *conj.*	since, as
(puisqu' before any vowel)	
sorte *f.n.*	manner, kind or sort
gros (*m.*), grosse (*f.*) *adj.*	bulky, fat
plusieurs *adj. & pl. pron.*	several
oublier	to forget
d'ailleurs *adv. phr.*	besides
lire	to read

je lis	nous lisons
tu lis	vous lisez
il, elle lit	ils, elles lisent

rue *f.n.*	road, street
rencontrer	to meet, come across
parfois *adv.*	occasionally
ouvrir	to open

j'ouvre	nous ouvrons
tu ouvres	vous ouvrez
il, elle ouvre	ils, elles ouvrent

cher (*m.*), chère (*f.*) *adj.*	dear (of price, in affection)

Unit 17

reconnaître	to recognise (conjugated like connaître)
œuvre *f.n.*	work
haut *adj.*	high, tall
parmi *prep.*	among, amid
suffire	to suffice
heureux (*m.*), heureuse (*f.*) *adj.*	happy
malgré *prep.*	in spite of
service *m.n.*	service
arrêter	to stop, arrest
lequel (*m.*), laquelle (*f.*) *pron.* (*pl.* lesquels, lesquelles)	who, whom, which
mauvais *adj.*	bad, evil
apprendre	to learn (conjugated like prendre)
maître *m.n.*	master
fort *adv.*	very, strongly
continuer	to continue
moyen *m.n.*	means

Unit 18

table *f.n.*	table
autour *adv.*	round, about (of place)
action *f.n.*	act, action
exister	to exist
face *f.n.*	face
fort *adj.*	strong
loi *f.n.*	law
point *adv.*	not at all
famille *f.n.*	family
route *f.n.*	road, way
expliquer	to explain
problème *m.n.*	problem
dessus *adv.*	above, on, over, top
nombre *m.n.*	number
soleil *m.n.*	sun
quitter	to vacate, leave
âme *f.n.*	soul, feeling
mort *f.n.*	death
chacun *pron.*	each one, every one
sujet *m.n.*	subject, cause

Unit 19

caractère *m.n.*	character, nature
plaisir *m.n.*	pleasure
autant *adv.*	as much (many), so much (many)
manquer	to lack, be short (Il me manque cent francs, I am 100 francs short)
situation *f.n.*	situation, position
nature *f.n.*	nature
fait *adj.*	ripe, developed
siècle *m.n.*	century
libre *adj.*	free
ordre *m.n.*	order
tomber	to fall
propre *adj.*	proper, clean, own
peuple *m.n.*	people, nation
mourir	to die

je meurs	nous mourons
tu meurs	vous mourez
il, elle meurt	ils, elles meurent

tard *adj.*	late
air *m.n.*	air
entier (*m.*), entière (*f.*) *adj.*	entire
plutôt *adv.*	rather, on the whole
souvenir *m.n.*	memory, memento
voix *f.n.*	voice

Unit 20

mère *f.n.*	mother
second *adj.*	second
considérer	to consider
jeu *m.n.*	game
(*pl.* jeux)	
poser	to set, rest, place
ligne *f.n.*	line
vraiment *adv.*	truly, really
noir *adj.*	black
époque *f.n.*	epoch
humain *adj.*	human
garder	to keep, preserve, observe
ciel *m.n.*	sky, heaven
(*pl.* cieux)	
apparaître	to appear (conjugated like paraître)
personne *f.n.*	person
assurer	to fix, secure, assure, insure
ajouter	to add
effort *m.n.*	effort, endeavour
tirer	to pull, pull off, shoot

Unit 21

argent *m.n.*	money, silver
attention *f.n.*	attention
	(Attention! Watch out!)
empêcher	to prevent, impede
journée *f.n.*	day, daytime
manière *f.n.*	manner, way
meilleur *adj.*	better
condition *f.n.*	condition (*pl.* terms)
changer	to change, exchange
bout *m.n.*	end, extremity
obtenir	to obtain
important *adj.*	important
semaine *f.n.*	week
instant *m.n.*	moment, instant
prix *m.n.*	price, value
monter	to climb, ascend
sûr *adj.*	sure
difficile *adj.*	difficult
salle *f.n.*	hall, (large) room
songer	to dream, imagine

Unit 22

travailler	to work (intransitive); torment (transitive)
demi *adj.*	half
paix *f.n.*	peace
sens *m.n.*	sense, direction
parole *f.n.*	word, speech
finir	to finish
goût *m.n.*	taste, style
intérêt *m.n.*	interest
différent *adj.*	different
mer *f.n.*	sea
remarquer	to observe, remark
début *m.n.*	first appearance, outset
pur *adj.*	pure
détail *m.n.*	detail, retail
tourner	to turn, revolve
pensée *f.n.*	thought
étude *f.n.*	study
air *m.n.*	appearance
jeter	to throw, cast
sentiment	feeling, opinion

Unit 23

nombreux (*m.*), nombreuse (*f.*) *adj.*	numerous
toucher	to touch
objet *m.n.*	object
ensemble *adv.*	together
occuper	to occupy, fill
minute *f.n.*	minute
verité *f.n.*	truth
honneur *m.n.*	honour
milieu *m.n.*	middle
essayer	to try, taste (wine)
chemin *m.n.*	way, road
étranger (*m.*), étrangère (*f.*) *adj.*	foreign, strange
lumière *f.n.*	light
auteur *m.n.*	author
découvrir	to discover, uncover
présence *f.n.*	presence
franc *m.n.*	franc (unit of currency)
fils *m.n.*	son, (with names) junior
accepter	to accept

Unit 24

résultat *m.n.*	result
payer	to pay
valoir	to be worth

je vaux	nous valons
tu vaux	vous valez
il, elle vaut	ils, elles valent

impossible *adj.*	impossible
âge *m.n.*	age
roi *m.n.*	king
représenter	to represent, portray
ancien (*m.*), ancienne (*f.*) *adj.*	ancient, old, former
descendre	to descend, dismount, alight
garçon *m.n.*	boy, bachelor, servant
existence *f.n.*	existence
espérer	to hope (*but* j'espère, I hope)
histoire *f.n.*	history
hier *adv.*	yesterday
grâce *f.n.*	grace, charm, thanks
personne *pron.*	anyone, no-one
apercevoir	to perceive, glimpse
mal *m.n.*	harm, evil, ailment
(*pl.* maux)	
ah! *interj.*	ah! oh!
retenir	to hold back, retain
	(conjugated like tenir)

Unit 25

posséder	to possess
bras *m.n.*	arm
pareil (*m.*), pareille (*f.*) *adj.*	similar, equal
écouter	to listen
lettre *f.n.*	letter
fleur *f.n.*	flower
société *f.n.*	society, club, company
feu *m.n.*	fire, heat
produire	to produce, yield
hôtel *m.n.*	hotel, mansion (*but* hôtel de ville, Town Hall)
facile *adj.*	easy
région *f.n.*	region, area
élever	to erect, raise (*but* j'élève, I raise)
travers *m.n.*	breadth, failing (de travers, askew)
guère *adv.*	not much
erreur *f.n.*	error, delusion
journal *m.n.* (*pl.* journaux)	newspaper, journal
courir	to run
je cours	nous courons
tu cours	vous courez
il, elle court	ils, elles courent
politique *f.n.*	policy, politics
pauvre *adj.*	poor

Unit 26

bord *m.n.*	board, side, edge
saint *m.n.*	saint
juger	to judge, adjudge, try (case)
vite *adv.*	quickly
liberté *f.n.*	freedom, liberty
imposer	to impose, enforce
cours *m.n.*	course, currency, quotation (money)
conduire	to conduct, drive
je conduis	nous conduisons
tu conduis	vous conduisez
il, elle conduit	ils, elles conduisent
cesser	to cease
scène *f.n.*	scene, stage
regard *m.n.*	look, gaze, glance
divers *adj.*	different, various
demain *adv.*	tomorrow
souffrir	to suffer, allow, undergo
rôle *m.n.*	rôle, roll, list
contraire *m.n.*	contrary
dur *adj.*	hard, tough
faute *f.n.*	fault, offence, lack, need
refuser	to refuse, fail
nécessaire *adj.*	necessary

Unit 27

remettre	to replace, send back, postpone (conjugated like mettre)
gouvernement *m.n.*	government
ensuite *adv.*	then, afterwards
rentrer	return, go/come in, go/come home
tandis que *conj.*	while, whereas
principe *m.n.*	principle
ignorer	to be ignorant, not to know
curieux (*m.*), curieuse (*f.*) *adj.*	curious, interested
départ *m.n.*	sorting, departure
simplement *adv.*	simply
demeurer	to remain, stay
grave *adj.*	heavy, severe, grave
haut *adv.*	above, up
observer	to observe, note, watch
former	to form, shape, train
après *adv.*	afterwards
difficulté *f.n.*	difficulty
compter	to count, charge
parfait *adj.*	perfect
imaginer	to imagine, think

Unit 28

rouge *adj.*	red
avant *adv.*	beforehand
rapport *m.n.*	report, relation, profit
manger	to eat
inutile *adj.*	useless
atteindre	to attain, reach, hit
habitude *f.n.*	custom, habit (d'habitude, usually)
appartenir	to belong (conjugated like tenir)
naturel (*m.*), naturelle (*f.*) *adj.*	natural
joie *f.n.*	joy, delight
impression *f.n.*	impression, print, exposure
chef *m.n.*	head, chief, leader
importance *f.n.*	importance
pas *m.n.*	step (faux pas, false step)
décider	to decide
profond *adj.*	deep, profound
champ *m.n.*	field
lever	to raise, lift
doux (*m.*), douce (*f.*) *adj.*	sweet, gentle, mild

Unit 29

école *f.n.*	school
particulier (*m.*), particulière (*f.*) *adj.*	private, particular, special
eh! *interj.*	hey!
dormir	to sleep
je dors	nous dormons
tu dors	vous dormez
il, elle dort	ils, elles dorment
voyage *m.n.*	journey, tour
bas (*m.*), basse (*f.*) *adj.*	low
réalité *f.n.*	reality
visage *m.n.*	face
clair *adj.*	clear, bright
présent *m.n.*	present, gift
acte *m.n.*	action, act
préparer	to prepare
confiance *f.n.*	confidence, trust
somme *f.n.*	sum, amount (*but* le somme, nap, snooze)
répéter	to repeat, rehearse (*but* je répète)
couleur *f.n.*	colour
régime *m.n.*	normal operation, form of government
vivant *adj.*	living
expression *f.n.*	expression
robe *f.n.*	dress, skin (of vegetable, etc.)

Unit 30

tendre	to stretch, tend, lead
politique *adj.*	political, shrewd
geste *m.n.*	gesture, movement (*but* la geste, exploit)
saisir	to seize
reste *m.n.*	remains
frapper	to strike, hit
selon *prep.*	according to
court *adj.*	short
intéresser	to interest
classe *f.n.*	class
moindre *adj.*	lesser (le, la moindre, least)
vent *m.n.*	wind
ministre *m.n.*	minister, servant
article *m.n.*	article
exprimer	to express
mur *m.n.*	wall
vif (*m.*), vive (*f.*) *adj.*	alive, living
hiver *m.n.*	winter
groupe *m.n.*	group

Unit 31

bureau *m.n.*	office, writing-desk, board
science *f.n.*	knowledge, science
pousser	to push
commun *adj.*	common
image *f.n.*	image
accord *m.n.*	agreement (d'accord! agreed!)
peur *f.n.*	fear (j'ai peur, I am afraid)
disposition *f.n.*	layout, disposition
projet *m.n.*	project, scheme
douter	to doubt
automobile *f.n.*	car (usually abbreviated to auto)
révéler	to reveal, betray (*but* je révèle)
bonheur *m.n.*	success, luck
réponse *f.n.*	answer, reply
qualité *f.n.*	quality, qualification
léger (*m.*), légère (*f.*) *adj.*	light, slight, gentle
évidemment *adv.*	evidently
disparaître	to disappear (conjugated like paraître)
envoyer	to send
j'envoie	nous envoyons
tu envoies	vous envoyez
il, elle envoie	ils, elles envoient
parti *m.n.*	party, course

Unit 32

oiseau *m.n.*	bird
(*pl.* oiseaux)	
rire	to laugh
je rie	nous rions
tu ríes	vous riez
il, elle rit	ils, elles rient
espèce *f.n.*	kind, sort
succès *m.n.*	success, result
examiner	to examine, scrutinise
période *f.n.*	period
annoncer	to announce
devoir	to have to, owe
je dois	nous devons
tu dois	vous devez
il, elle doit	ils, elles doivent
signe *m.n.*	sign, symbol
constituer	to form, constitute
silence *m.n.*	silence
public (*m.*), publique (*f.*) *adj.*	public
établir	to establish, draw up
histoire *f.n.*	story
figure *f.n.*	figure, face
domaine *m.n.*	domain, field
véritable *adj.*	real, true
bois *m.n.*	wood, forest
chien (*m.*), chienne (*f.*) *n.*	dog
amener	to bring (about), convey
	(*but* j'amène, I bring)

Unit 33

naître	to be born
je nais	nous naissons
tu nais	vous naissez
il, elle naît	ils, elles naissent
frère *m.n.*	brother
constater	to ascertain, state
artiste *m. & f.n.*	artist, performer
puissance *f.n.*	power, strength
admettre	to admit, allow
large *adj.*	broad, wide, ample
pouvoir *m.n.*	power, force
armée *f.n.*	army
déclarer	to declare
conserver	to preserve, retain
soin *m.n.*	care, attention
échapper	to escape
marcher	to go, travel, march
supérieur *adj.*	upper, superior
usine *f.n.*	works, factory
occasion *f.n.*	occasion, opportunity
dame *f.n.*	lady
traiter	to treat
étonner	to stun, astonish

Unit 34

distinguer	to distinguish, characterise
poursuivre	to pursue (conjugated like suivre)
musique *f.n.*	music
église *f.n.*	church
mener	to lead, drive, steer (*but* je mène)
usage *m.n.*	use, usage, wear
riche *adj.*	rich
amitié *f.n.*	friendship, friendliness
immense *adj.*	huge, immense
créer	to create
titre *m.n.*	title
cri *m.n.*	cry, shout
combien *adv.*	how much, how many
verre *m.n.*	glass
complet (*m.*), complète (*f.*) *adj.*	complete, full up
village *m.n.*	village
compagnie *f.n.*	company
retour *m.n.*	return, reversal

Unit 35

mademoiselle *f.n.* (*pl.* mesdemoiselles)	miss
convenir	to suit, admit, fit (conjugated like venir)
page *f.n.*	page
chaud *adj.*	hot
gagner	to earn, gain, win
allemand *adj.*	German
aspect *m.n.*	sight, aspect
supposer	to suppose, assume
parent (*m.*), parente (*f.*) *n.*	parent, relative
ailleurs *conj.*	elsewhere
raconter	to tell, narrate
voiture *f.n.*	car, cart, van
matière *f.n.*	matter, material
plaire	to please

je plais	nous plaisons
tu plais	vous plaisez
il, elle plaît	ils, elles plaisent

papier *m.n.*	paper
plupart *f.n.*	majority, greater part
métier *m.n.*	trade, profession
adresser	to address (s'adresser ici, apply here)
membre *m.n.*	member
troisième *adj.*	third

Unit 36

hasard *m.n.*	chance, luck, accident
battre	to beat

je bats	nous battons
tu bats	vous battez
il, elle bat	ils, elles battent

or *conj.*	now, but, well
théâtre *m.n.*	theatre, drama
foi *f.n.*	faith
oser	to dare
jardin *m.n.*	garden
brillant *adj.*	brilliant
ouvert *adj.*	open
autorité *f.n.*	authority
prêter	to lend, attribute
volonté *f.n.*	will
or *m.n.*	gold
choisir	to choose
merveilleux (*m.*), merveilleuse (*f.*) *adj.*	marvellous
placer	to set, place
attitude *f.n.*	behaviour, attitude
genre *m.n.*	genre, kind, manner
système *m.n.*	system

Unit 37

proposer	to propose
événement *m.n.*	event, incident
derrière *prep.*	behind
marche *f.n.*	step, walking (en marche, in motion)
bientôt *adv.*	soon (a bientôt! so long!)
réussir	to result, succeed
méthode *f.n.*	method
capable *adj.*	capable
avenir *m.n.*	future
marquer	to mark, score, show
défendre	to defend
exactement *adv.*	exactly
cheval *m.n.* (*pl.* chevaux)	horse
prétendre	to claim, assert
but *m.n.*	object, aim, goal
précis *adj.*	exact, accurate
maintenir	to maintain (conjugated like tenir)
passé *m.n.*	past
élément *m.n.*	element

Unit 38

également *adv.*	equally, likewise
comme *conj.*	as, seeing that
faux (*m.*), fausse (*f.*) *adj.*	false
relever	to raise, hold up (conjugated like lever)
tour *m.n.*	trip, tour, turn
réaliser	to realise, carry out
naturellement *adv.*	of course, naturally
froid *adj.*	cold
traverser	to cross, pass through
bleu *adj.*	blue
marché *m.n.*	market, deal
importer	to matter, be important
désirer	to desire, wish
voie *f.n.*	way, track
auprès *adv.*	close to
accorder	to reconcile, grant
économique *adj.*	economic
arbre *m.n.*	tree
américain	American

Unit 39

courant *m.n.*	current, stream
faible *adj.*	feeble, weak
concerner	to concern
actuel (*m.*), actuelle (*f.*) *adj.*	present, current
pierre *f.n.*	stone
davantage *adv.*	more
nu *adj.*	naked, bare
souhaiter	to wish
pluie *f.n.*	rain
ramener	to bring back (conjugated like mener)
défaut *m.n.*	lack, absence, default
cacher	to hide
prêt *adj.*	ready, prepared
chanter	to sing
conscience *f.n.*	conscience, consciousness
lourd *adj.*	heavy, dull
émotion *f.n.*	emotion
prononcer	to pronounce
aussitôt *adv.*	immediately
étoile *f.n.*	star

Unit 40

comporter	to comprise, require, call for
rare *adj.*	rare
tuer	to kill
soldat *m.n.*	soldier
propos *m.n.*	subject, purpose
craindre	to fear
partout *adv.*	everywhere
fer *m.n.*	iron
terme *m.n.*	term, end
social *adj.*	social
(*pl.* sociaux)	
sang *m.n.*	blood
boire	to drink
je bois	nous buvons
tu bois	vous buvez
il, elle boit	ils, elles boivent
joli *adj.*	pretty
terminer	to end, bring to an end
poète (*m.*), femme poète	poet
or poétesse (*f.*) *n.*	
fin *adj.*	fine
été *m.n.*	summer
ressembler	to resemble
charmant *adj.*	charming

Unit 41

droit *adj.*	right
devoir *m.n.*	duty, exercise (homework)
activité *f.n.*	activity
souvenir	to remember, recall (conjugated like venir)
aventure *f.n.*	adventure
connaissance *f.n.*	knowledge, acquaintance
public *m.n.*	public, people
intéressant *adj.*	interesting
avouer	acknowledge, admit
justice *f.n.*	justice
bruit *m.n.*	noise, rumour
souci *m.n.*	care, worry
crise *f.n.*	crisis, attack (of nerves, etc.)
nord *m.n.*	north
complètement *adv.*	completely
espoir *m.n.*	hope
abandonner	to abandon
lit *m.n.*	bed
énorme *adj.*	huge, enormous
supporter	to support, endure

Unit 42

beauté *f.n.*	beauty
passage *m.n.*	passage, crossing, flow
faveur *f.n.*	favour
pris *adj.*	occupied, busy
neige *f.n.*	snow
parvenir	to reach, arrive at (conjugated like venir)
quelquefois *adv.*	sometimes
centre *m.n.*	centre
moral *adj.* (*pl.* moraux)	moral
employer	to employ
fameux (*m.*), fameuse (*f.*) *adj.*	famous
parfaitement *adv.*	perfectly
secret *m.n.*	secret
fournir	to supply
contenir	to contain (conjugated like tenir)
ouvrier (*m.*), ouvrière (*f.*) *n.*	worker
figurer	to represent, imagine, figure
tableau *m.n.* (*pl.* tableaux)	board, painting, table

Unit 43

bas *adv.*	low down
militaire *adj.*	military
docteur *m.n.*	doctor
changement *m.n.*	change
diriger	to direct, control, run
vaste *adj.*	vast
camarade *m. & f.n.*	comrade
national *adj.*	national
certes *adv.*	certainly, to be sure
circonstance *f.n.*	circumstance, event
fenêtre *f.n.*	window
fermé *adj.*	closed
jeunesse *f.n.*	youth
mort *adj.*	dead
oh! *interj.*	oh!
pénétrer	to penetrate
sol *m.n.*	ground, earth
cependant *adv.*	meanwhile
intérieur *adj.*	inner, internal
mari *m.n.*	husband
particulièrement *adv.*	particularly

Unit 44

visite *f.n.*	visit
ton *m.n.*	tone, breeding, manners
commerce *m.n.*	commerce, trade
éviter	to avoid
froid *m.n.*	cold
présent *adj.*	present
bouche *f.n.*	mouth
cependant *conj.*	yet, nevertheless
moderne *adj.*	modern
professeur *m.n.*	professor, teacher
conversation *f.n.*	conversation
après-midi *m.n.*	afternoon
égard *m.n.*	regard, respect
utile *adj.*	useful
droite *f.n.*	right-hand
maladie *f.n.*	illness, disease
trait *m.n.*	flash, stroke
bien *m.n.*	possession, good (biens, goods)
unique *adj.*	only, sole
réfléchir	to reflect, ponder

Unit 45

soi *pron.*	oneself, himself, herself, itself
principal *adj.* (*pl.* principaux)	principal, main
chance *f.n.*	chance, luck
président *m.n.*	president
crime *m.n.*	crime
prochain *adj.*	next, nearest
conclure	to conclude
montagne *f.n.*	mountain
net (*m.*), nette (*f.*) *adj.*	clean, clearcut
opinion *f.n.*	opinion
sec (*m.*), sèche (*f.*) *adj.*	dry
fermer	to close
rêve *m.n.*	dream
patron (*m.*), patronne (*f.*) *n.*	patron, master, employer
épreuve *f.n.*	proof, test
nul (*m.*), nulle (*f.*) *adj.*	non-existent, no

Unit 46

dehors *adv.*	outside
coin *m.n.*	corner, nook
étendre	to stretch, enlarge
témoin *m.n.*	witness
habiter	to inhabit, live in
magnifique *adj.*	magnificent
vin *m.n.*	wine
triste *adj.*	sad
crier	to shout, cry
foule *f.n.*	crowd, crush
absolument *adv.*	absolutely
réel (*m.*), réelle (*f.*) *adj.*	real
ouvrage *m.n.*	work, product
éprouver	to prove, test
excellent *adj.*	excellent
subir	to suffer, undergo
suivant *adj.*	next, following
campagne *f.n.*	plain, countryside, campaign
acheter	to buy
ceci *pron.*	this

Unit 47

soit *conj.*	whether, either
position *f.n.*	position
palais *m.n.*	palace, palate
accompagner	to accompany
lèvre *f.n.*	lip
durer	to last
juste *adj.*	just, right
salon *m.n.*	drawing-room, salon, saloon
remplacer	to replace
terrain *m.n.*	ground, land
spectacle *m.n.*	spectacle, entertainment, show
étudier	to study
ennemi *m.n.*	enemy
signaler	to report, mark
désormais *adv.*	henceforth
prouver	to prove
repos *m.n.*	rest, repose
saison *f.n.*	season
reposer	to rest, replace
plan *m.n.*	plan, drawing, plane

Unit 48

citer	to quote, cite, summon
précisément *adv.*	precisely
général *m.n.*	general
(*pl.* généraux)	
tôt *adv.*	soon
mariage *m.n.*	wedding, marriage
retirer	to retire, take back
fonction *f.n.*	function
preuve *f.n.*	evidence, proof
puissant *adj.*	powerful, strong
atmosphère *f.n.*	atmosphere
séparer	to separate
endroit *m.n.*	place, side
directeur (*m.*), directrice (*f.*) *n.*	director, directress
tromper	to deceive, betray (se tromper, to be mistaken)
envie *f.n.*	desire, envy
intérieur *m.n.*	interior (à l'intérieur, inside)
attirer	to attract, draw
sœur *f.n.*	sister

Unit 49

source *f.n.*	source, spring, origin
moitié *f.n.*	half
mémoire *f.n.*	memory, recollection
sauf *prep.*	save, except
sourire	to smile (conjugated like rire)
personnel (*m.*), personnelle (*f.*) *adj.*	personal
dépasser	to go beyond, overtake
soutenir	to support, sustain (conjugated like tenir)
personnage *m.n.*	personage, character
délicat *adj.*	sensitive, delicate
sauver	to save, preserve
passion *f.n.*	passion
apparence *f.n.* (N.B. spelling)	appearance
danger *m.n.*	danger
semblable *adj.*	like, similar
quant à *prep.*	with regard to
misère *f.n.*	misery
phénomène *m.n.*	phenomenon
autrement *adv.*	otherwise, differently

Unit 50

cheveu *m.n.*
   (*pl.* cheveux)

one hair, *pl.* the hair as a whole

inspirer — to inspire

santé *f.n.* — health

château *m.n.*
   (*pl.* châteaux)

castle, palace

province *f.n.* — province

mériter — to merit, deserve

surprise *f.n.* — surprise

vendre — to sell

avion *m.n.* — aeroplane, aircraft (par avion, by airmail)

premier (*m.*), première (*f.*) *n.* — first (occasion), première

fou (*m.*), folle (*f.*) *adj.* — mad, crazy

masse *f.n.* — mass

disposer — to dispose, lay out

origine *f.n.* — origin, descent

appel *m.n.* — appeal, call

revoir — to see again, meet again (conjugated like voir)

Unit 51

formule *f.n.*	form, formula
prier	to beg, pray (je vous en prie! please do!)
peau *f.n.* (*pl.* peaux)	skin, hide
malheureux (*m.*), malheureuse (*f.*) *adj.*	unhappy
développer	to stretch out, unroll, develop
désir *m.n.*	wish, desire
révolution *f.n.*	revolution
ensemble *m.n.*	whole, unity
quartier *m.n.*	district, quarter
sérieux (*m.*), sérieuse (*f.*) *adj.*	serious
avis *m.n.*	notice, advice, opinion
rapidement *adv.*	quickly
aider	to help, assist
prince *m.n.*	prince
front *m.n.*	forehead, front
billet *m.n.*	ticket, letter, bill
considérable *adj.*	considerable
anglais *adj.*	English, British
insister	to insist

Unit 52

aussi *conj*.	so, consequently
assister	to help (assister à, to attend, be present at)
tenter	to tempt, attempt
bateau *m.n.* (*pl.* bateaux)	boat
lendemain *m.n.*	day after, next day
fixer	to fix, assess
quelqu'un (*m.*), quelqu'une (*f.*) *pron.*	somebody, one (*pl.* quelques-un(e)s, a few)
million *m.n.*	million
livrer	to deliver, surrender
opération *f.n.*	operation
rapporter	to report, bring back, withdraw
extérieur *adj*.	external, exterior
arrivée *f.n.*	arrival
regretter	to regret
indiquer	to indicate, lay down
arme *f.n.*	weapon
taire	to suppress, hush up (se taire, to be silent)
extraordinaire *adj*.	extraordinary
entretenir	to maintain, entertain (conjugated like tenir)

Unit 53

dent *f.n.*	tooth
commettre	to commit, risk (conjugated like mettre)
relation *f.n.*	relation, report
confier	to trust, entrust, confide
soudain *adv.*	suddenly
exiger	to require, call for, exact
installer	to install, equip
intention *f.n.*	intention
pleurer	to weep, mourn for
résoudre	to solve, resolve, settle
éclat *m.n.*	to clap, flash, splinter
pain *m.n.*	bread
illusion *f.n.*	illusion
remonter	to re-ascend, go up again
défense *f.n.*	defence, prohibition
réduire	to reduce
solution *f.n.*	solution
étrange *adj.*	strange, odd
entraîner	to entail, carry along
brusquement *adv.*	abruptly

Unit 54

agent *m.n.*	agent
dit *adj.*	said, fixed, settled
éloigner	to remove, send away
mort *m.n.*	dead (person) (cf. la mort, death)
entourer	to encircle, surround
jadis *adv.*	formerly
attacher	to attach, bind
soirée *f.n.*	evening, reception, party
dimanche *m.n.*	Sunday
approcher	to approach
économie *f.n.*	economics, economy
gauche *f.n.*	left-hand side
production *f.n.*	production
déposer	to put down, deposit, depose
printemps *m.n.*	Spring
tantôt *adv.*	soon, just now
lecture *f.n.*	reading
précédent *adj.*	preceding
perdu *adj.*	lost
texte *m.n.*	text

Unit 55

passé *adj.*	past
engager	to engage, start, involve, entangle
étage *m.n.*	storey, rank
avancer	to advance, put forward
mètre *m.n.*	metre
entrée *f.n.*	entrance, admission
extrême *adj.*	extreme, utmost
fortune *f.n.*	fortune, luck
coucher	to put to bed (se coucher, to go to bed)
série *f.n.*	series, succession
affirmer	to assert, affirm
règle *f.n.*	rule
tort *m.n.*	error, wrong, injury
notion *f.n.*	notion, idea
asseoir	to set, pitch (s'asseoir, to sit down, conjugated below)

je m'assois (assieds)	nous vous asseyons
tu t'assois (assieds)	vous vous asseyez
il, elle s'assoit (assied)	ils, elles s'assoient

courage *m.n.*	courage
prévoir	to foresee, provide for (conjugated like voir, except future and conditional tenses)
vertu *f.n.*	valour, virtue, chastity
charger	to charge, load, burden
flamme *f.n.*	flame, passion

Unit 56

peintre *m.n.*	painter
frais (*m.*), fraîche (*f.*) *adj.*	fresh, cool
rêver	to dream, dream of
gare *f.n.*	station
explication *f.n.*	explanation
train *m.n.*	train, noise
admirable *adj.*	admirable
énergie *f.n.*	energy
forêt *f.n.*	forest
estimer	to estimate, esteem
médecin *m.n.*	(medical) doctor
français *m.n.*	Frenchman
imagination *f.n.*	imagination
précieux (*m.*), précieuse (*f.*) *adj.*	precious, affected
conséquence *f.n.*	consequence (par conséquent, en conséquence, consequently)
direction *f.n.*	conduct, management, direction
degré *m.n.*	step, degree
chargé *adj.*	loaded, charged

Unit 57

malade *m. & f.n.*	invalid, sick person
phrase *f.n.*	sentence, (musical) phrase
administration *f.n.*	administration, governing body
autrefois *adv.*	formerly
lait *m.n.*	milk
exercer	to exercise, practise (a trade)
officier *m.n.*	officer
réserve *f.n.*	reserve, reservation
conception *f.n.*	conception, idea
avantage *m.n.*	advantage
port *m.n.*	port, carriage (of post, of a person)
expérience *f.n.*	experience, experiment
quart *m.n.*	quarter
sensible *adj.*	sensitive, perceptible
contact *m.n.*	contact
transformer	to transform
veille *f.n.*	staying up, watch, eve
tradition *f.n.*	tradition
sinon *conj.*	otherwise, if not
fête *f.n.*	festival, show

Unit 58

empire *m.n.*	authority, sway, empire
conseil *m.n.*	council, counsel, plan
terrible *adj.*	terrible
quantité *f.n.*	quantity
long *m.n.*	length
donné *adj.*	given
promener	to take for a walk (*but* je promène) (se promener, go for a walk)
hélas! *interj.*	alas!
revue *f.n.*	review, inspection, magazine
officiel (*m.*), officielle (*f.*) *adj.*	official
obliger	to force, compel, oblige
vide *adj.*	empty
toutefois *adv.*	nevertheless, yet
humeur *f.n.*	humour, temper
concevoir	to conceive, understand
je conçois	nous concevons
tu conçois	vous concevez
il, elle conçoit	ils, elles conçoivent
produit *m.n.*	product
certainement *adv.*	certainly
gloire *f.n.*	glory
portrait *m.n.*	portrait, face
banque *f.n.*	bank

Unit 59

génie *m.n.*	genius, engineering
promettre	to promise
	(conjugated like mettre)
vert *adj.*	green
progrès *m.n.*	progress
mise *f.n.*	setting, placing
exposer	to exhibit, display, expose
spécial *adj.*	special
victime *f.n.*	victim
poussière *f.n.*	dust
reprocher	to reproach, grudge
curiosité *f.n.*	curiosity
clef *f.n.*	key
appartement *m.n.*	flat, apartment, room
malade *adj.*	sick, ill
nommer	to name
type *m.n.*	type, character, fellow
vitesse *f.n.*	speed
emporter	to carry, carry away
international *adj.*	international
photographie *f.n.*	photograph, photography

Unit 60

céder	to give way, yield (*but* je cède)
oreille *f.n.*	ear
amant (*m.*), amante (*f.*) *n.*	lover
rapide *adj.*	rapid, swift
crédit *m.n.*	credit
deviner	to predict, guess
distance *f.n.*	distance
colonie *f.n.*	colony
race *f.n.*	race, breed, ancestry
partager	to share, divide
dos *m.n.*	back
élève *m. & f.n.*	student, pupil
civilisation *f.n.*	civilisation
ombre *f.n.*	shade, shadow
noter	to note
influence *f.n.*	influence
physique *adj.*	physical
avance *f.n.*	lead, advance, projection
secret (*m.*), secrète (*f.*) *adj.*	secret

Unit 61

base *f.n.*	base, basis
marchand (*m.*), marchande (*f.*) *n.*	shopkeeper, tradesperson
matériel (*m.*), matérielle (*f.*) *adj.*	material, materialistic
réveiller	to awake, arouse (se réveiller, to wake oneself up)
célèbre *adj.*	famous, celebrated (*with* par, for)
mêler	to mingle, mix, shuffle
propriétaire *m. & f.n.*	proprietor, proprietress; landlord, landlady
retourner	to return, go back
prison *f.n.*	imprisonment, prison
doigt *m.n.*	finger
angoisse *f.n.*	anguish, distress
risquer	to risk
digne *adj.*	worthy, deserving (*with* de, of)
proposition *f.n.*	proposal, proposition
nouvelle(s) *f.n.*	piece of news, (news)
définitif (*m.*), définitive (*f.*) *adj.*	permanent, definitive
publier	to publish
bête *f.n.*	beast, blockhead

Unit 62

interroger	to examine, interrogate
statue *f.n.*	statue
animal *m.n.*	animal
(*pl.* animaux)	
outre *adv.*	further (en outre, besides)
film *m.n.*	film
organiser	to organise
rencontre *f.n.*	encounter, meeting, occasion
manifester	to show, evince, manifest
richesse *f.n.*	wealth
sacré *adj.*	holy, sacred
style *m.n.*	style
population *f.n.*	population
cour *f.n.*	court, courtyard
connu *adj.*	well-known, acquainted
intelligence *f.n.*	understanding, intelligence
troupe *f.n.*	troupe, throng, herd, troop
immédiatement *adv.*	immediately
chapitre *m.n.*	chapter, item
obligé *adj.*	compelled, indispensable, grateful

Unit 63

achever	to complete, conclude (*but* j'achève)
langage *m.n.*	language, speech
arracher	to snatch, pull away, tear out
intime *m. & f.n.*	intimate friend
contenter	to gratify, satisfy
nécessité *f.n.*	necessity
arrière *adv.*	behind, backwards (*more usually* en arrière)
préférer	to prefer (*but* je préfère)
éclater	to burst, flash, splinter
chair *f.n.*	flesh, pulp
lentement *adv.*	slowly
chasse *f.n.*	hunt, hunting
sonner	to strike, sound, ring
date *f.n.*	date (in time; *the fruit is* la datte)
leçon *f.n.*	lesson
réunir	to convene, reunite
tranquille *adj.*	calm
chapeau *m.n.* (*pl.* chapeaux)	hat
responsabilité *f.n.*	responsibility
profiter	to take advantage (*with* de, of)

Unit 64

discours *m.n.*	talk, speech, language
inconnu *adj.*	unknown
développement *m.n.*	development
ministère *m.n.*	ministry, agency
renoncer	to renounce, give up
hors *pron.*	outside, out of
différence *f.n.*	difference
procéder	to proceed, act (conjugated like céder: je cède)
jugement *m.n.*	judgement
recueillir	to gather, collect (conjugated like cueillir)
odeur *f.n.*	odour, scent
glace *f.n.*	ice
étroit *adj.*	narrow, tight
composer	to compose, make up
poésie *f.n.*	poetry, poem
nôtre *pron.* (*pl.* nôtres)	ours
embrasser	to embrace, kiss, include
appareil *m.n.*	appliance, machine, display
reine *f.n.*	queen
détruire	to destroy

Unit 65

dépit *m.n.*	spite, resentment (en dépit de, in spite of)
cabinet *m.n.*	office, small room, cabinet
hésiter	to hesitate, falter
horreur *f.n.*	horror
précision *f.n.*	precision, accuracy
fier (*m.*), fière (*f.*) *adj.*	proud
accomplir	to accomplish, carry out
épaule *f.n.*	shoulder
manteau *m.n.* (*pl.* manteaux)	cloak, coat
introduire	to introduce
observation *f.n.*	observation
réellement *adv.*	really, actually
serrer	to shake, clasp, put away
équilibre *m.n.*	balance, stability
résister	to resist, withstand
normal *adj.* (*pl.* normaux)	normal, standard
consister	to consist
larme *f.n.*	tear (en larmes, in tears)
dégager	to disengage, release, redeem
voisin *adj.*	neighbouring, next

Unit 66

neuf (*m.*), neuve (*f.*) *adj.*	new
sud *m.n.*	south
admirer	to admire
conclusion *f.n.*	conclusion
drame *m.n.*	drama, play
universel (*m.*), universelle (*f.*) *adj.*	universal
tâche *f.n.*	task
commander	to command, order, control
placé *adj.*	placed
évident *adj.*	obvious
malheur *m.n.*	accident, misfortune
police *f.n.*	police, policy
cesse *f.n.*	ceasing (sans cesse, unceasingly)
rechercher	to search for, enquire into
total *adj.*	total
fleuve *m.n.*	river
récent *adj.*	recent
presse *f.n.*	press, pressure
inviter	to invite

Unit 67

poids *m.n.*	weight
honte *f.n.*	shame
écarter	to brush aside, separate, dismiss
couvert *adj.*	covered
jaune *adj.*	yellow
désordre *m.n.*	disorder
discussion *f.n.*	discussion, argument
privé *adj.*	private
île *f.n.*	island
déterminer	to decide, determine
vague *adj.*	vague, dim
surpris *adj.*	surprised
impôt *m.n.*	tax
bloc *m.n.*	bloc, block
poule *f.n.*	hen
douleur *f.n.*	pain, sorrow
lancer	to throw, launch, start
note *f.n.*	note, mark
appuyer	to support, press
lune *f.n.*	moon

Unit 68

entendu *adj.*	understood
menace *f.n.*	menace
étranger (*m.*), étrangère (*f.*) *n.*	foreigner, stranger
réclamer	to complain, claim
cadre *m.n.*	frame, framework, cadre
branche *f.n.*	branch
organisation *f.n.*	organisation
solide *adj.*	solid
scientifique *adj.*	scientific
appliquer	to apply
création *f.n.*	creation
absence *f.n.*	absence
balle *f.n.*	ball, bullet
afin de *prep.*	in order to
capitaine *m.n.*	captain
enlever	to carry off, away (*but* j'enlève)
application *f.n.*	application
fixe *adj.*	fixed
juge *m.n.*	judge, magistrate, umpire

Unit 69

rayon *m.n.*	ray, radius, spoke
opposer	to oppose
remercier	to thank
dangereux (*m.*), dangereuse (*f.*) *adj.*	dangerous
mesurer	to measure
parisien (*m.*), parisienne (*f.*) *adj.*	Parisian
respirer	to breathe
manœuvre *f.n.*	manœuvre, drill, driving
industrie *f.n.*	industry
séjour *m.n.*	stay, abode
individu *m.n.*	individual (person)
financier (*m.*), financière (*f.*) *adj.*	financial
indispensable *adj.*	indispensable
modeste *adj.*	modest
consacrer	to consecrate, devote
ressource *f.n.*	resource
fini *adj.*	finished

Unit 70

lors (= alors) *adv.*	when (lors de sa arrivée, when he arrived)
intervenir	to intervene, interfere (conjugated like venir)
fruit *m.n.*	fruit
lecteur (*m.*), lectrice (*f.*) *n.*	reader
dresser	to make out, set out, prepare
violent *adj.*	violent
désigner	to design
midi *m.n.*	midday, south (après midi, afternoon)
résistance *f.n.*	resistance
quelconque *adj.*	any
dîner *m.n.*	dinner
naissance *f.n.*	birth
ressentir	to resent, feel (conjugated like sentir)
fidèle *adj.*	faithful
évoquer	to evoke
remplir	to fill, complete
provoquer	to provoke, cause
motif *m.n.*	motive, reason
mérite *m.n.*	merit, worth

Unit 71

recommencer	to start again
pitié *f.n.*	pity
chiffre *m.n.*	figure, amount, cipher
heureusement *adv.*	happily
aide *f.n.*	aid, rescue, relief
	(*m. & f.n.*, helper)
grandeur *f.n.*	size, greatness, splendour
propriété *f.n.*	property, ownership
atelier *m.n.*	studio, workshop
exception *f.n.*	exception
venu *adj.*	come
sucre *m.n.*	sugar
promenade *f.n.*	walk, walking, stroll
aborder	to land, berth, accost
culture *f.n.*	culture
justement *adv.*	properly, precisely
vers *m.n.*	verse, line
russe *adj.*	Russian
dessous *adv.*	beneath, below
garde *f.n.*	guard, care, watchman
carrière *f.n.*	career, racecourse
suprême *adj.*	supreme

Unit 72

station *f.n.*	station
actuellement *adv.*	at the present time
enfance *f.n.*	childhood
glisser	to slide, slip
mystérieux (*m.*), mystérieuse (*f.*) *adj.*	mysterious
herbe *f.n.*	grass, herb
réflexion *f.n.*	reflection, thought
exact *adj.*	exact, true, punctual
peinture *f.n.*	paint, painting
soumettre	to submit, subject (conjugated like mettre)
pont *m.n.*	bridge
absolu *adj.*	absolute
territoire *m.n.*	territory
demeure *f.n.*	residence, delay
industriel (*m.*), industrielle (*f.*) *adj.*	industrial
seigneur *m.n.*	lord, nobleman
colère *f.n.*	anger
favorable *adj.*	favourable
choix *m.n.*	choice

Unit 73

dominer	to rule, dominate, overcome
langue *f.n.*	tongue, language
proche *adj.*	near
fil *m.n.*	thread, wire, edge
inventer	to invent
sommeil *m.n.*	sleep, sleepiness
union *f.n.*	union, unity
couvrir	to cover
historique *adj.*	historic, historical
accident *m.n.*	accident
instinct *m.n.*	instinct
régler	to rule, regulate (*but* je règle)
charge *f.n.*	burden, office, expense
association *f.n.*	association
excès *m.n.*	excess
vis-à-vis *prep.*	with regard to
folie *f.n.*	madness
possession *f.n.*	possession
critique *f.n.*	criticism, review
satisfaire	to satisfy
	(conjugated like faire)

Unit 74

tendre *adj.*	tender, soft
interdire	to forbid, disconcert
cinéma *m.n.*	cinema, films
définir	to define
	(conjugated like finir)
caisse *f.n.*	fund, cash, till, case
combat *m.n.*	fight, contest
pièce *f.n.*	piece, room, play
fantaisie *f.n.*	fancy, imagination
religieux (*m.*), religieuse (*f.*) *adj.*	religious
vœu *m.n.* (*pl.* vœux)	vow, wish
hommage *m.n.*	tribute, homage
aboutir	to succeed, lead to, result in
paysage *m.n.*	landscape
lampe *f.n.*	light, lamp
plaindre	to pity (se plaindre, to complain)
décret *m.n.*	decree
chaise *f.n.*	chair
gauche *adj.*	left, clumsy

Unit 75

ranger	to arrange, tidy away
tendance *f.n.*	tendency, trend
vain *adj.*	vain
monument *m.n.*	monument
littérature *f.n.*	literature
course *f.n.*	race, running, excursion
incapable *adj.*	incapable, inefficient
retard *m.n.*	delay (en retard, late)
entreprise *f.n.*	business, untertaking
dehors *m.n.*	exterior, outside
mince *adj.*	slender, thin
construire	to construct, build, assemble
respect *m.n.*	respect, regard
cercle *m.n.*	circle
tour *f.n.*	tower
revanche *f.n.*	revenge (en revanche, on the other hand)
choc *m.n.*	impact, clash, shock
pénible *adj.*	laborious, painful
soulever	to raise, arouse (conjugate like lever; je soulève)
réaction *f.n.*	reaction

Unit 76

poche *f.n.*	pocket, bag
dîner	to dine
obscur *adj.*	dark, obscure, humble
vrai *m.n.*	truth, right
foyer *m.n.*	hearth, fire, focus
élevé *adj.*	exalted, high, lofty
machine *f.n.*	engine, machine
document *m.n.*	document
sombre *adj.*	dim, gloomy
affreux (*m.*), affreuse (*f.*) *adj.*	hideous, frightful
rejoindre	to catch up, reunite (conjugated like joindre)
mystère *m.n.*	mystery
épais (*m.*), épaisse (*f.*) *adj.*	thick
tendresse *f.n.*	tenderness
nouveau *m.n.*	item of news (du nouveau, something new)
gaz *m.n.*	gas
inquiétude *f.n.*	unease, anxiety
secours *m.n.*	help, assistance
précaution *f.n.*	precaution

Unit 77

épouser	to marry
modèle *m.n.*	pattern, model
lent *adj.*	slow
idéal *m.n.*	ideal
(*pl.* idéals *or* idéaux)	
renseignement *m.n.*	an item of information (usually *pl.* des renseignements, some information)
établi *adj.*	established
comédie *f.n.*	comedy, play
considéré *adj.*	considered, respected
décembre *m.n.*	December
pardonner	to pardon
risque *m.n.*	risk
roman *m.n.*	novel
rire *m.n.*	laughter
durée *f.n.*	wear, duration
tache *f.n.*	stain, blemish
démontrer	to demonstrate
abri *m.n.*	shelter
consommation *f.n.*	consumption, drink, expenditure
boîte *f.n.*	box, night-club
direct *adj.*	direct, straight

Unit 78

constant *adj.*	constant
trou *m.n.*	hole
prière *f.n.*	prayer, request
croix *f.n.*	cross
couper	to cut
agréable *adj.*	agreeable
régulier (*m.*), régulière (*f.*) *adj.*	regular
feuille *f.n.*	leaf, sheet
arranger	to arrange (s'arranger, to manage)
consacré *adj.*	consecrated, established
délicieux (*m.*), délicieuse (*f.*) *adj.*	delicious
jambe *f.n.*	leg
transport *m.n.*	transport
kilomètre *m.n.*	kilometre
relatif (*m.*), relative (*f.*) *adj.*	relative
lien *m.n.*	tie, bond
rond *adj.*	round
déclaration *f.n.*	declaration
crainte *f.n.*	fear
surprendre	to surprise

Unit 79

sommet *m.n.*	summit
singulier (*m.*), singulière (*f.*) *adj.*	singular
transformation *f.n.*	transformation
client (*m.*), cliente (*f.*) *n.*	client
août *m.n.*	August
café *m.n.*	coffee, coffee-house
décor *m.n.*	decoration, décor
préparation *f.n.*	preparation
çà *adv.*	hither (çà et là, hither and thither)
limite *f.n.*	boundary, limit
escalier *m.n.*	stairs, staircase
varié *adj.*	varied
pratique *f.n.*	practice, application
plante *f.n.*	plant, sole of the foot
écrivain *m.n.*	writer, author
particulier (*m.*), particulière (*f.*) *n.*	private person, individual
danser	to dance
sympathie *f.n.*	sympathy, attraction
république *f.n.*	republic
rapprocher	to draw near, bring together

Unit 80

traité *m.n.*	treaty, treatise
finance *f.n.*	finance
volontiers *adv.*	willingly
dessin *m.n.*	drawing, design
sauter	to jump, change, explode
talent *m.n.*	talent
double *adj.*	double
possibilité *f.n.*	possibility
nez *m.n.*	nose
programme *m.n.*	programme
essai *m.n.*	trial, test, essay
religion *f.n.*	religion
établissement *m.n.*	establishment
lutte *f.n.*	struggle, wrestling
navire *m.n.*	ship
échange *m.n.*	exchange
patte *f.n.*	foot (of bird), paw (of animal)
miracle *m.n.*	miracle
boulevard *m.n.*	boulevard, rampart
proportion *f.n.*	proportion

Unit 81

coûter	to cost
brouillard *m.n.*	mist
éloigné *adj.*	far off, remote
hauteur *f.n.*	height, arrogance
député *m.n.*	deputy, delegate
emploi *m.n.*	use, employment
haine *f.n.*	hatred
opérer	to operate, perform (*but* j'opère)
triomphe *m.n.*	triumph
accuser	to accuse, show, own up to
évolution *f.n.*	evolution
soigner	to tend, look after
nettement *adv.*	clearly, cleanly
numéro *m.n.*	number
bref (*m.*), brève (*f.*) *adj.*	brief, short
interrompre	to interrupt
régiment *m.n.*	regiment
généralement *adv.*	generally
couple *m.n.*	couple, pair
sort *m.n.*	destiny, chance, spell

Unit 82

téléphoner	to telephone
spirituel (*m.*), spirituelle (*f.*) *adj.*	spiritual
reprise *f.n.*	resumption, recapture, stage in sport (round, bout, second half)
intelligent *adj.*	intelligent
représentant (*m.*), représentante (*f.*) *n.*	representative
heurter	to knock, run into
morceau *m.n.* (*pl.* morceaux)	bit, piece, morsel of food
nullement *adv.*	not at all, by no means
septembre *m.n.*	September
exceptionnel (*m.*), exceptionnelle (*f.*) *adj.*	exceptional
pratique *adj.*	practical
musée *m.n.*	museum
humanité *f.n.*	humanity, human nature
jouir	to enjoy
repousser	to reject, recoil, repel (conjugated like pousser)
classique *adj.*	classical
rejeter	to reject, throw back, cast up (conjugated like jeter)
juste *adv.*	rightly, exactly
allusion *f.n.*	allusion

Unit 83

fonds *m.n.*	fund, funds, means
anglais (*m.*), anglaise (*f.*) *n.*	English person
cou *m.n.*	neck
profit *m.n.*	profit
commercial *adj.*	commercial
(*pl.* commerciaux)	
secrétaire *m. & f.n.*	secretary
ferme *adj.*	firm, steady
discuter	to discuss, argue
collection *f.n.*	collection
amuser	to amuse, entertain
vigueur *f.n.*	vigour (en vigueur, in force)
prétexte *m.n.*	pretext
indépendant *adj.*	independent
(N.B. spelling)	
bénéfice *m.n.*	profit, benefit
trésor *m.n.*	treasure
parfum *m.n.*	perfume
démarche *f.n.*	step, gait
vide *m.n.*	void, vacuum, empty space
terrasse *f.n.*	terrace, pavement (outside a café)

Unit 84

rideau *m.n.* (*pl.* rideaux)	curtain
cité *f.n.*	city
facilement *adv.*	easily
aile *f.n.*	wing
résumer	to summarise
goutte *f.n.*	drop, sip
entièrement *adv.*	entirely
calme *adj.*	calm
carte *f.n.*	map, card, sheet of paper
utiliser	to use
enthousiasme *m.n.*	enthusiasm
content *adj.*	satisfied, pleased
frontière *f.n.*	frontier
écrit *adj.*	written
visiter	to visit
professionnel (*m.*), professionnelle (*f.*) *adj.*	professional
rose *f.n.*	rose
obéir	to obey

Unit 85

prévenir	to anticipate, avert, inform (conjugated like venir)
parcourir	to travel through, skim (conjugated like courir)
chasseur (*m.*), chasseuse (*f.*) *n.*	hunter, huntress
recouvrir	to recover, cover (conjugated like couvrir)
ange *m.n.*	angel
fonctionnaire *m.n.*	official, civil servant
chasser	to hunt, chase, drive away
correspondre	to correspond
fusil *m.n.*	gun
préciser	to state, specify
pointe *f.n.*	point, peak
divin *adj.*	divine
costume *m.n.*	costume
troubler	to trouble, confuse, muddy
laine *f.n.*	wool
presser	to press, squeeze, hurry on
cuisine *f.n.*	cooking, kitchen
gré *m.n.*	liking, will
dû (*m.*), due (*f.*) *adj.*	due, owing
essentiel (*m.*), essentielle (*f.*) *adj.*	essential

Unit 86

harmonie *f.n.*	harmony, agreement
proclamer	to proclaim
durant *prep.*	during
univers *m.n.*	universe
dommage *m.n.*	damage (Quel dommage! What a pity!)
conférence *f.n.*	conference, lecture
petit (*m.*), petite (*f.*) *n.*	child, young (of an animal)
consentir	to consent (conjugated like sentir)
faiblesse *f.n.*	weakness, failing
situé *adj.*	situated
accent *m.n.*	accent, tone
poste *m.n.*	post, station (*not* sense of 'mail')
notamment *adv.*	notably
sacrifier	to sacrifice
examen *m.n.*	examination
peser	to weigh (*but* je pèse)
bain *m.n.*	bath
maîtresse *f.n.*	mistress
cadavre *m.n.*	corpse, carcase
princesse *f.n.*	princess

Unit 87

nerveux (*m.*), nerveuse (*f.*) *adj.*	nervous
argument *m.n.*	argument, summary
rude *adj.*	uncouth, rough, harsh
écrier	to cry out
retraite *f.n.*	retirement, retreat
occupé *adj.*	to occupy, employ, inhabit
entretien *m.n.*	upkeep, maintenance, interview
congrès *m.n.*	congress
décisif (*m.*), décisive (*f.*) *adj.*	decisive
fièvre *f.n.*	fever
fatigué *adj.*	tired
surveiller	to supervise, look after
excuser	to excuse (someone) (s'excuser, to excuse oneself)
instruction *f.n.*	lesson, training
précéder	to precede (conjugated like céder, i.e. je précède)
victoire *f.n.*	victory
réservé *adj.*	reserved, shy
adopter	to adopt
exercice *m.n.*	exercise

Unit 88

allonger	to lengthen
destinée *f.n.*	destiny
debout *adv.*	upright
né *adj.*	born
bande *f.n.*	band, strip, flock
procurer	to obtain
dépense *f.n.*	expense, dispensary
confirmer	to confirm
huile *f.n.*	oil
briser	to break, smash
surface *f.n.*	surface
faim *f.n.*	hunger
choisi *adj.*	chosen
personnalité *f.n.*	personality
bataille *f.n.*	battle
voyageur (*m.*), voyageuse (*f.*) *n.*	traveller
édifice *m.n.*	building
signifier	to mean
philosophie *f.n.*	philosophy

Unit 89

œuf *m.n.*	egg
nourrir	to nourish, rear, maintain
médiocre *adj.*	mediocre
exécuter	to perform, execute
toit *m.n.*	roof
tellement *adv.*	so
regret *m.n.*	regret
dépendre	to depend, belong to
mensonge *m.n.*	lie
catégorie *f.n.*	category
éclairer	to light, instruct
confondre	to confuse, baffle
pressé *adj.*	crowded, hurried
comte *m.n.*	count (French), earl (English)
répandre	to pour out, spread, scatter
construction *f.n.*	building, construction
éternel (*m.*), éternelle (*f.*) *adj.*	eternal
gêner	to inconvenience, obstruct
continu *adj.*	continuous
mission *f.n.*	mission

Unit 90

réserver	to reserve
brusque *adj.*	abrupt, sudden
capital *m.n.*	capital (money)
(*pl.* capitaux)	
majorité *f.n.*	majority
organisme *m.n.*	organism
épargner	to save, be sparing
rigueur *f.n.*	rigour, severity (de rigueur, obligatory)
attaque *f.n.*	attack
magasin *m.n.*	shop, warehouse
pencher	to lean, incline
incident *m.n.*	incident
user	to use
département *m.n.*	department, ministry
royal *adj.*	royal
représentation *f.n.*	representation, performance, exhibition
humide *adj.*	humid, damp
transporter	to transport, transfer
reproche *m.n.*	reproach
ouest *m.n.*	west
destin *m.n.*	destiny

Unit 91

tissu *m.n.*	material, texture
suffisant *adj.*	sufficient
colonne *f.n.*	column, pillar
coupé *adj.*	cut (up), broken
goûter	to taste, enjoy
mecanique *adj.*	mechanical
maman *f.n.*	mummy
fatigue *f.n.*	fatigue
charbon *m.n.*	coal, carbon
apprécier	to value, estimate, appreciate
souffle *m.n.*	breath
charme *m.n.*	charm
emmener	to lead away, take away (*but* j'emmène)
coutume *f.n.*	custom, habit
bassin *m.n.*	basin, dock, bowl
isolé *adj.*	isolated
fluir	to flee, avoid
complexe *adj.*	complex
souffrance *f.n.*	suffering, suspense
forcer	to force

Unit 92

douceur *f.n.*	gentleness, sweetness
composé *adj.*	composite, compound
génération *f.n.*	generation
boue *f.n.*	mud, dirt
éteindre	to put out, switch off (conjugated like teindre)
conseiller	to counsel, recommend
liaison *f.n.*	liaison
lointain *adj.*	distant
sou *m.n.*	(colloquially) penny (je suis sans le sou, I am broke)
régner	to reign
permanent *adj.*	permanent
enseignement *m.n.*	teaching, tuition
exposition *f.n.*	exhibition, statement
saluer	to greet
perte *f.n.*	loss, destruction
extrêmement *adv.*	extremely
infini *adj.*	infinite
convention *f.n.*	convention
honnête *adj.*	honest, decent
probable *adj.*	probable

Unit 93

confus *adj.*	confused
rendez-vous *m.n.*	appointment, meeting-place
vente *f.n.*	sale
juillet *m.n.*	July
obligation *f.n.*	obligation, bond
douloureux (*m.*), douloureuse (*f.*) *adj.*	sad, painful
témoigner	to bear witness, prove
conduite *f.n.*	conduct, direction, driving
moteur *m.n.*	motor, engine
variété *f.n.*	variety
sûrement *adv.*	surely, safely
quai *m.n.*	quay, embankment, platform
delà *adv.*	beyond
quoique *conj.*	though, although
consulter	to consult
quotidien (*m.*), quotidienne (*f.*) *adj.*	daily
contrôle *m.n.*	checkpoint, inspection, test
actif (*m.*), active (*f.*) *adj.*	active

Unit 94

savant (*m.*), savante (*f.*) *n.*	scholar, scientist
inférieur *adj.*	lower, inferior
toilette *f.n.*	toilet, washing and dressing
tâcher	to strive, try
bleu *n.*	blue
uniquement *adv.*	solely, simply
fixé *adj.*	fixed
perfection *f.n.*	perfection
mentir	to lie
réjouir	to delight, entertain (conjugated like jouir)
plat *m.n.*	dish, course, flat (of racing, tyres)
courant *adj.*	current, flowing, running
déjeuner *m.n.*	lunch
contribuer	to contribute
probablement *adv.*	probably
assis *adj.*	seated
profondément *adv.*	deeply, profoundly
décision *f.n.*	decision
plage *f.n.*	beach, sea resort

Unit 95

noble *adj.*	noble
trace *f.n.*	track, trace
chat (*m.*), chatte (*f.*) *n.*	cat
éveiller	to wake up
diable *m.n.*	devil
populaire *adj.*	popular
conquérir	to conquer
réunion *f.n.*	assembly, reunion
tragique *adj.*	tragic
débarrasser	to clear, rid
endormir	to put to sleep, bore (s'endormir, to fall asleep)
remarquable *adj.*	remarkable
étendu *adj.*	extended, outstretched
niveau *m.n.* (*pl.* niveaux)	level
formation *f.n.*	education, formation
merveille *f.n.*	wonder
violence *f.n.*	violence
chute *f.n.*	fall
néanmoins *conj.*	yet, nevertheless
profondeur *f.n.*	depth

Unit 96

jurer	to swear
souffler	to breathe, pant, blow
drôle *adj*.	funny, odd
merci *m.n*.	thanks
.sac *m.n*.	bag, sack
tapis *m.n*.	carpet, cover
brun *adj*.	brown
modification *f.n*.	modification
infiniment *adv*.	infinitely
température *f.n*.	temperature
chauffeur (*m*.), chauffeuse (*f*.) *n*.	driver, stoker
inscription *f.n*.	inscription
traduire	to translate, summon, indict
savant *adj*.	erudite, skilful
acquérir	to acquire, obtain (*but* j'acquiers)
volume *m.n*.	volume
concert *m.n*.	concert, agreement
légitime *adj*.	legitimate
comparer	to compare
assemblée *f.n*.	assembly

Unit 97

miroir *m.n.*	mirror
chant *m.n.*	song, singing
janvier *m.n.*	January
horrible *adj.*	horrible
modifier	to modify
manque *m.n.*	lack, shortage
armé *adj.*	armed, equipped
mépris *m.n.*	contempt
tombe *f.n.*	tomb
prolonger	to prolong, extend
unité *f.n.*	unit, unity
allumer	to light, inflame
commission *f.n.*	commission, errand
nier	to deny
épuiser	to exhaust, sell out
rivière *f.n.*	river
lutter	to fight, struggle
lac *m.n.*	lake
débattre	to debate, discuss (conjugated like battre)
éclairé *adj.*	lit, well-informed

Unit 98

écraser	to crush, squash, overwhelm
plainte *f.n.*	complaint, groan, legal action
évidence *f.n.*	evidence, obviousness
protéger	to protect (*but* je protège)
toile *f.n.*	cloth, linen, oil painting
alcool *m.n.*	alcohol
commencement *m.n.*	beginning
sagesse *f.n.*	wisdom
communiquer	to communicate, infect
architecte *m.n.*	architect
indifférent *adj.*	indifferent, insensible, immaterial
horizon *m.n.*	horizon
transmettre	to transmit
justifier	to justify
réputation *f.n.*	reputation
subtil *adj.*	subtle, delicate, shrewd
réalisé *adj.*	realised, carried out
chanson *f.n.*	song
sacrifice *m.n.*	sacrifice
samedi *m.n.*	Saturday

Unit 99

longuement *adv.*	slowly, for a long time
allemand *m.n.*	German
posé *adj.*	calm, grave, steady
espace *m.n.*	space, distance
intimité *f.n.*	intimacy, depths
accueillir	to receive, greet (conjugated like cueillir)
primitif (*m.*), primitive (*f.*) *adj.*	primitive, primary
académie *f.n.*	academy
genou *m.n.* (*pl.* genoux)	knee
original *adj.* (*pl.* originaux)	original
recommander	to recommend, register
contrat *m.n.*	contract, agreement
récit *m.n.*	story, account
blanc *m.n.*	white
directement *adv.*	directly
tristesse *f.n.*	sadness
échec *m.n.*	check, setback
adversaire *m.n.*	opponent
délivrer	to deliver

Unit 100

audace *f.n.*	audacity
trouble *m.n.*	disturbance, trouble
inspecteur (*m.*), inspectrice (*f.*) *n.*	inspector
vérifier	to check, confirm, verify
distinction *f.n.*	distinction
forcé *adj.*	forced, compulsory
orgueil *m.n.*	pride
parc *m.n.*	park
orient *m.n.*	Orient
résolution *f.n.*	resolution
calme *m.n.*	calm(ness)
immédiat *adj.*	immediate
viande *f.n.*	meat, food
italien (*m.*), italienne (*f.*) *adj.*	Italian
accrocher	to hook, run into
colline *f.n.*	hill
fumer	to smoke
ardent *adj.*	burning, passionate

French Index

chose 6
chute 95
ci 14
ci-el, -eux 20
cinéma 73
circonstance 43
cité 84
citer 48
civilisation 60
clair 29
classe 30
classique 82
clef 59
client 79
cœur 13
coin 46
colère 72
collection 83
colline 100
colonie 60
colonne 91
combat 74
combien 34
comédie 77
commander 66
comme 3, 38
commencement 98
commencer 12
comment 13
commerce 44
commerci-al, -aux 83
commettre 53
commission 97
commun 31
communiquer 98
compagnie 34
comparer 96
compl-et, -ète 34
complètement 41
complexe 91
comporter 40
composé 92
composer 64
comprendre 9
compte 14
compter 27
comte 89
conception 57
concerner 39

concert 96
concevoir 58
conclure 45
conclusion 66
condition 21
conduire 26
conduite 93
conférence 86
confiance 29
confier 53
confirmer 88
confondre 89
confus 93
congrès 87
connaissance 41
connaître 8
connu 62
conquérir 95
consacré 78
consacrer 69
conscience 39
conseil 58
conseiller 92
consentir 86
conséquence 56
conserver 33
considérable 51
considéré 77
considérer 20
consister 65
consommation 77
constant 78
constater 33
constituer 32
construction 89
construire 75
consulter 93
contact 57
contenir 42
content 84
contenter 63
continu 89
continuer 17
contraire 26
contrat 99
contre 10
contribuer 94
contrôle 93
convenir 35

convention 92
conversation 44
corps 14
correspondre 85
costume 85
côté 11
cou 83
coucher 55
couleur 29
coup 11
coupé 91
couper 78
couple 81
cour 62
courage 55
courant 39, 94
courir 25
cours 26
course 75
court 30
coûter 81
coutume 91
couvert 67
couvrir 73
craindre 40
crainte 78
création 68
crédit 60
créer 34
cri 34
crier 46
crime 45
crise 41
critique 73
croire 5
croix 78
cuisine 85
culture 71
curi-eux, -euse 27
curiosité 59

d'accord 31
dame 33
danger 49
danger-eux, -euse 69
dans 2
danser 79

écouter 25
écraser 98
écrier 87
écrire 15
écrit 84
écrivain 79
édifice 88
effet 13
effort 20
également 38
égard 44
église 34
eh! 29
élément 37
élevé 76
élève 60
élever 25
elle/s 1
éloigné 81
éloigner 54
embrasser 64
emmener 91
émotion 39
empêcher 21
empire 58
emploi 81
employer 42
emporter 59
en 2, 3
encore 4
endormir 95
endroit 48
énergie 56
enfance 72
enfant 9
enfin 9
engager 55
enlever 68
en marche 37
ennemi 47
énorme 41
enseignement 92
ensemble 23, 51
ensuite 27
entendre 13
entendu 68
enthousiasme 84
enti-er, -ère 19
entièrement 84

entourer 54
entraîner 53
entre 6
entrée 55
entreprise 75
entrer 13
entretenir 52
entretien 87
envie 48
envoyer 31
épais/se 76
épargner 90
épaule 65
époque 20
épouser 77
épreuve 45
éprouver 46
épuiser 97
equilibre 65
erreur 25
escalier 79
espace 99
espèce 32
espérer 24
espoir 41
esprit 13
essai 80
essayer 23
essentiel/le 85
estimer 56
et 1
établi 77
établir 32
établissement 80
étage 55
état 14
été 40
éteindre 92
étendre 46
étendu 95
eternel/le 89
étoile 39
étonner 33
étrange 53
étrang-er, -ère 23, 68
être 1
étroit 64
étude 22
étudier 47

eux 3
éveiller 95
événement 37
évidemment 31
évidence 98
évident 66
éviter 44
évolution 81
évoquer 70
exact 72
exactement 37
examen 86
examiner 32
excellent 46
exception 71
exceptionel/le 82
excès 73
excuser 87
exécuter 89
exemple 14
exercer 57
exercice 87
exiger 53
existence 24
exister 18
expérience 57
explication 56
expliquer 18
exposer 59
exposition 92
expression 29
exprimer 30
extérieur 52
extraordinaire 52
extrême 55
extrêmement 92

face 18
facile 25
facilement 84
façon 12
faible 39
faiblesse 86
faim 88
faire 3
fait 9, 19
falloir 4

lune 67
lutte 86
lutter 97

ma 3
machine 76
madame 11
mademoiselle 35
magasin 90
magnifique 46
main 12
maintenant 10
maintenir 37
mais 2
maison 10
maître 17
maîtresse 86
majorité 90
mal 16, 24
malade 57, 59
maladie 44
malgré 17
malheur 66
malheur-eux, -euse 51
maman 91
manger 28
manière 21
manifester 62
manœuvre 69
manque 97
manquer 19
manteau/x 65
marchand 61
marche 37
marché 38
marcher 33
mari 43
mariage 47
marquer 37
masse 50
matériel/le 61
matière 35
matin 12
mauvais 17
maux 24
me 3
mecanique 91

médecin 56
médiocre 89
meilleur 21
mêler 61
membre 35
même 4, 5
mémoire 49
mener 34
mensonge 89
mentir 94
mépris 97
mer 22
merci 96
mère 20
mérite 70
mériter 50
merveille 95
merveill-eux, -euse 36
mes 3
mesdemoiselles 35
messieurs 4
mesure 15
mesurer 69
méthode 37
métier 35
mettre 6
midi 70
mieux 10
milieu 23
militaire 43
million 52
mince 75
ministère 64
ministre 30
minute 23
miracle 80
miroir 97
mise 59
misère 49
mission 89
modèle 77
moderne 44
modeste 69
modification 96
modifier 97
moi 6
moindre 30
moins 5
mois 12

moitié 49
moment 8
mon 3
monde 8
monsieur 4
montagne 45
monter 21
montrer 11
monument 75
mor-al, -aux 42
morceau/x 82
mort 18, 43, 54
mot 10
moteur 93
motif 70
mourir 19
mouvement 14
moyen 17
mur 30
musée 82
musique 34
mystère 76
mystéri-eux, -euse 72

naissance 70
naître 33
nation-al, -aux 43
nature 19
naturel/le 28
naturellement 38
navire 80
ne 1
né 88
néanmoins 95
nécessaire 26
necessité 63
neige 42
nerv-eux, -euse 87
net/te 45
nettement 81
n-euf, -euve 66
nez 80
ni 8
nier 97
niveau/x 95
noble 95
noir 20

nom 11
nombre 18
nombr-eux, -euse 23
nommer 59
non 5
nord 41
norm-al, -aux 65
nos 4
notamment 86
note 67
noter 60
notion 55
notre 4
nôtre 64
nourrir 89
nouveau/x 8, 76
nouvel/le/s 8, 61
nu 39
nuit 12
nul/le 45
nullement 82
numéro 81

obéir 84
objet 23
obligation 93
obligé 62
obliger 58
obscur 76
observation 65
observer 27
obtenir 21
occasion 33
occupé 87
occuper 23
odeur 64
œil 8
œuf 89
œuvre 17
officiel/le 58
officier 57
offrir 16
oh! 43
oiseau/x 32
ombre 60
on 2
opération 52

opérer 81
opinion 45
opposer 69
or 36
ordre 19
oreille 60
organisation 68
organiser 62
organisme 90
orgueil 100
orient 100
origin-al, -aux 99
origine 50
oser 36
ou 3
où 3
oublier 16
ouest 90
oui 15
outre 62
ouvert 36
ouvrage 46
ouvr-ier, -ière 42
ouvrir 16

page 35
pain 53
paix 22
palais 47
papier 35
par 2
paraître 8
par avion 50
parc 100
parce que 9
parcourir 85
pardonner 77
pareil 25
parent 35
parfait 27
parfaitement 42
parfois 16
parfum 83
parisien/ne 69
parler 6
parmi 17
parole 22

part 11
partager 60
parti 31
particul-ier, -ière, 29, 79
particulièrement 43
partie 14
partir 13
partout 40
parvenir 42
pas 2, 28
passage 42
passé 37, 55
passer 7
passion 49
patron/ne 45
patte 80
pauvre 25
payer 24
pays 11
paysage 74
peau/x 51
peintre 56
peinture 72
pencher 90
pendant 10
pénétrer 43
pénible 75
pensée 22
penser 8
perdre 14
perdu 54
père 15
perfection 94
période 32
permanent 92
permettre 10
personnage 49
personnalité 88
personne 20, 24
personnel/le 49
perte 92
peser 86
petit 5, 86
peu 4
peuple 19
peur 31
peut-être 9
phénomène 49
philosophie 88

quand 5
quant à 49
quantité 58
quart 57
quartier 51
que 1
quelconque 70
quel/le 7
quelque 4
quelquefois 42
quelqu'un 52
question 11
qui 2
quitter 18
quoi 12
quoique 93
quotidien/ne 93

race 60
raconter 35
raison 14
ramener 39
ranger 75
rapid 60
rapidement 51
rappeler 14
rapport 28
rapporter 52
rapprocher 79
rare 40
rayon 69
réaction 75
réalisé 98
réaliser 38
réalité 29
récent 66
recevoir 12
rechercher 66
récit 99
réclamer 68
recommander 99
recommencer 71
reconnaître 17
recouvrir 85
recueillir 64
réduire 53
réel/le 46

réellement 65
réfléchir 44
réflexion 72
refuser 26
regard 26
regarder 13
régime 29
régiment 81
région 25
règle 55
régler 73
régner 92
regret 89
regretter 52
reguli-er, -ère 78
reine 64
rejeter 82
rejoindre 76
rejouir 94
relat-if, -ive 78
relation 53
relever 38
religi-eux, -euse 74
remarquable 95
remarquer 22
remercier 69
remettre 27
remonter 53
remplacer 47
remplir 70
rencontre 62
rencontrer 16
rendez-vous 93
rendre 15
renoncer 64
renseignement 77
rentrer 27
répandre 89
répéter 29
répondre 14
réponse 31
repos 47
reposer 47
repousser 82
reprendre 15
représentant 82
représentation 90
représenter 24
reprise 82

reproche 90
reprocher 59
république 79
réputation 98
réserve 57
réservé 87
réserver 90
résistance 70
résister 65
résolution 100
résoudre 53
respect 75
respirer 69
responsabilité 63
ressembler 40
ressentir 70
ressource 69
reste 30
rester 7
résultat 24
résumer 84
retard 75
retenir 24
retirer 48
retour 34
retourner 61
retraite 87
retrouver 14
réunion 95
réunir 63
réussir 37
revanche 75
rêve 45
réveiller 61
révéler 31
revenir 10
rêver 56
revoir 50
révolution 51
revue 58
riche 34
richesse 62
rideau/x 84
rien 5
rigueur 90
rire 32, 77
risque 77
risquer 61
rivière 97

112

surveiller 87
sympathie 79
système 36

table 18
tableau/x 42
tache 77
tâche 66
tâcher 94
taire 52
talent 80
tandis que 27
tant 9
tantôt 54
tapis 96
tard 19
tel/le 8
téléphoner 82
tellement 89
témoigner 93
témoin 46
température 96
temps 5
tendance 75
tendre 30, 74
tendresse 76
tenir 7
tenter 52
terme 40
terminer 40
terrain 47
terrasse 83
terre 12
terrible 58
territoire 72
tête 12
texte 54
théâtre 36
tirer 20
tissu 91
titre 34
toile 98
toilette 94
toit 89
tombe 97
tomber 19
ton 44

tort 55
tôt 48
total 66
toucher 23
toujours 5
tour 38, 75
tourner 22
tous 2
tout 2, 4, 6
toutefois 58
trace 95
tradition 57
traduire 96
tragique 95
train 56
trait 44
traité 80
traiter 33
tranquille 63
transformation 79
transformer 57
transmettre 98
transport 78
transporter 90
travail 10
travailler 22
travers 25
traverser 38
très 4
trésor 83
triomphe 81
triste 46
tristesse 99
troisième 35
tromper 48
trop 7
trou 78
trouble 100
troubler 85
troupe 62
trouver 5
tuer 40
type 59

un 1
union 73
unique 44

uniquement 94
unité 97
univers 86
universel/le 66
usage 34
user 90
usine 33
utile 44
utiliser 84

vague 67
vain 75
valeur 15
valoir 24
varié 79
variété 93
vaste 43
veille 57
vendre 50
venir 4
vent 30
vente 93
venu 71
vérifier 100
véritable 32
verité 23
verre 34
vers 9, 71
vert 59
vertu 55
viande 100
victime 59
victoire 87
vide 58, 83
vie 6
vieil/le 10
vieux 10
v-if, -ive 30
vigueur 83
village 34
ville 12
vin 46
violence 95
visage 29
vis-à-vis 73
visite 44
visiter 84

English Index

by 2
by no means 82

cabinet 65
cadre 68
called, be 12
call 12, 50
calm 63, 84, 99
calmness 100
campaign 46
capable 37
capital 90
captain 68
car 31, 35
carbon 91
carcase 86
card 84
care 33, 41, 71
career 71
carpet 96
carriage 57
carry 11, 59
carry along 53
carry away 59, 68
carry off 68
carry out 38, 65, 98
cart 35
case 12, 74
cash 74
cast 22
castle 50
cast up 82
cat 95
catch up 76
category 89
cause 13, 18, 70
cease 26
ceasing 66
celebrated 61
centre 42
century 19
certain 7
certainly 43, 58
chair 74
chance 36, 45, 81
change 14, 21, 43, 80
chapter 62

character 19, 49, 59
characterise 34
charge 27, 55
charged 56
charm 24, 91
charming 40
chase 85
chastity 55
check 99, 100
checkpoint 93
chief 28
child 9, 86
childhood 72
choice 72
choose 36
chosen 88
church 34
cinema 74
cipher 71
circle 75
circumstance 43
cite 48
city 84
civilisation 60
civil servant 85
claim 37, 68
clap 53
clash 75
clasp 65
class 30
classical 82
clean 19, 45
cleanly 81
clear 29, 95
clearcut 45
clearly 81
client 79
climb 21
cloak 65
close 45
closed 43
close to 38
cloth 98
club 25
clumsy 74
coal 91
coat 65
coffee 79
coffee-house 79

cold 38, 44
collect 64
collection 83
colony 60
colour 29
column 91
come 4, 9, 71
come across 16
comedy 77
come home 27
come in 27
command 66
commerce 44
commercial 83
commission 97
commit 53
common 31
communicate 98
company 25, 34
compare 96
compel 58
compelled 62
complain 68, 74
complaint 98
complete 34, 63, 70
completely 41
complex 91
compose 64
composite 92
compound 92
comprise 40
compulsory 100
comrade 43
conceive 58
conception 57
concern 39
concert 96
conclude 45, 63
conclusion 66
condition 21
conduct 26, 64, 93
conference 86
confide 53
confidence 29
confirm 88, 100
confuse 85, 89
confused 93
congress 87
conquer 95

determine 67
develop 51
developed 19
development 64
devil 95
devote 69
die 19
difference 64
different 22, 26
differently 49
difficult 21
difficulty 27
dim 67, 76
dine 76
dinner 70
direct 43, 77
direction 22, 56, 93
directly 99
direct-or, -ress 48
dirt 92
disappear 31
disconcert 74
discover 23
discuss 83, 97
discussion 67
disease 44
disengage 65
dish 94
dismiss 67
dismount 24
disorder 67
dispensary 88
display 59, 64
dispose 50
disposition 31
distance 60, 99
distant 92
distinction 100
distinguish 34
distract 51
distress 61
district 11
disturbance 100
divide 60
divine 85
do 3
dock 91
doctor 43, 56
document 76

dog 32
domain 32
dominate 73
door 14
double 80
doubt 11, 31
drama 36, 66
draw 48
drawing 47, 80
drawing-room 47
draw near 79
draw up 32
dream 21, 45, 56
dress 29
dressing 94
drill 69
drink 40, 77
drive 26, 34
driver 96
driving 69, 93
drop 84
dry 45
due 85
dull 39
duration 77
during 10, 86
dust 59
duty 41

each 8
each one 18
ear 60
earl 89
early as, as 13
earn 35
earth 12, 43
easily 84
easy 15, 25
eat 28
economic 38
economics 54
economy 54
edge 26, 73
education 95
effect 13
effort 20
egg 89

either 47
element 37
elsewhere 35
embankment 93
embrace 64
emotion 39
empire 58
employ 42, 87
employer 45
employment 81
empty 58
empty space 83
encircle 54
encounter 62
end 14, 21, 40
end, bring to an 40
endeavour 20
endure 41
enemy 47
energy 56
enforce 26
engage 55
engine 76, 93
engineering 59
English 51
English person 83
enjoy 82, 91
enlarge 46
enormous 41
enough 8
enquire into 66
entail 53
entangle 55
enter 13
entertain 52, 83, 94
entertainment 47
enthusiasm 84
entire 19
entirely 4, 84
entrance 55
entrust 53
envy 48
epoch 20
equal 25
equally 38
equip 53
equipped 97
erect 25
errand 97

former 24
formerly 54, 57
formula 51
fortune 55
frame 68
framework 68
franc 23
free 19
freedom 26
French 13
Frenchman 56
fresh 56
friend 12, 63
friendliness 34
friendship 34
frightful 76
from there 3
front 51
frontier 84
fruit 70
full 15
full up 34
function 48
fund 74, 83
funny 96
further 62
future 37

gain 35
gait 83
game 20
garden 36
gas 76
gate 14
gather 64
gaze 26
general 14, 48
generally 81
generation 92
genius 59
genre 36
gentleman 4
gentleness 92
German 35, 99
gesture 30
get out 14
gift 29

girl 9, 15
give 4
give back 15
give up 64
given 58
give way 60
glance 26
glass 34
glimpse 24
gloomy 76
glory 58
go 6, 14, 33
goal 37
go back 61
god 14
go home 27
go in 27
gold 36
good 6, 44
goods 44
governing body 57
government 27, 29
grace 24
grant 38
grass 72
grateful 62
gratify 63
grave 27, 99
great 4
greatness 71
green 59
greet 92, 99
groan 98
ground 43, 47
group 30
grudge 59
guard 71
guess 60
gun 85

habit 28, 91
hair 50
half 22, 49
half, second 82
hall 21
hand 12
handsome 7

happily 71
happy 17
hard 26
harm 24
harmony 86
harsh 87
hat 63
hatred 81
have 1
have to 4, 32
he 1, 6
head 12, 28
health 50
heart 13
hearth 76
heat 25
heaven 20
heavy 27, 39
height 81
help 51, 52, 76
helper 71
hen 67
henceforth 47
her 3
herb 72
herd 62
here 3, 7, 14
hers 2
herself 2, 45
hesitate 65
hey! 29
hide 39, 51
hideous 76
high 17, 76
hill 100
him 3
himself 2, 45
his 2
historic/al 73
history 24
hit 28, 30
hither 79
hold 7
hold back 24
hold up 38
hole 78
holy 62
homage 74
homework 41

meeting 62
meeting place 93
member 35
memento 19
memory 19, 49
menace 68
men and women 13
merely 9
merit 50, 70
method 37
metre 55
midday 70
middle 23
mild 28
military 43
milk 57
million 52
mingle 61
minister 30
ministry 64, 90
minute 23
miracle 80
mirror 97
misery 49
misfortune 66
miss 35
mission 89
mist 81
Mister (Mr) 4
mistress (Mrs) 11, 86
mix 61
model 77
modern 44
modest 69
modification 96
modify 97
moment 8, 21
money 21
month 12
monument 75
moon 67
moral 42
more 2, 39
morning 12
morsel 82
mother 20
motion, in 37
motive 70
motor 93

mountain 45
mourn for 53
mouth 44
movement 14, 30
much 8
much, how 34
much, not 25
much, so 5, 9
much, too 25
mud 92
muddy 85
mummy 91
museum 82
music 34
my 3
mysterious 72
mystery 76

naked 39
name 11, 59
nap 29
narrate 35
narrow 64
nation 19
national 43
natural 28
naturally 38
nature 19
near 11, 73
nearest 45
nearly 11
necessary 26
necessary, be 4
necessity 63
neck 83
need 14, 26
neighbouring 65
neither 8
nervous 87
never 6
nevertheless 16, 44, 58, 95
new 8, 66, 76
news 61, 76
newspaper 25
next 10, 45, 46, 65
nice 6
night 12

night-club 77
no 5, 45
noble 95
nobleman 72
noise 41, 56
non-existent 45
nook 46
no one 9, 24
nor 8
normal 65
north 41
nose 80
not 1, 2, 5
notably 86
not at all 18, 82
note 27, 60, 67
nothing 5
notice 51
notion 55
nourish 89
novel 77
now 10, 36
number 18, 81
numerous 23

obey 84
object 23, 37
obligation 93
obligatory 90
oblige 58
obscure 76
observation 65
observe 20, 22, 27
obstruct 89
obtain 21, 88, 96
obvious 66
obviousness 98
occasion 33, 62
occasionally 16
occupied 42
occupy 23, 87
occurrence 9
odd 53, 96
odour 64
of 1
of course 38
offence 26

offer 16
office 31, 65, 73
officer 57
official 58, 85
of it 3
often 11
of the 1
of them 3
oh! 24, 43
oil 88
oil painting 98
old 24
on 2, 18
one 1, 2
one's 2
oneself 2, 45
only 6, 9, 44
open 16, 36
operate 81
operation 52
opinion 22, 45, 51
opponent 99
opportunity 33
oppose 69
or 3
order 19, 66
order to, in 68
organisation 68
organise 62
organism 90
Orient 100
origin 49, 50
original 99
other 5, 7
other hand, on the 75
otherwise 49, 57
our 4
ours 64
out of 64
outset 22
outside 46, 64, 75
outstretched 95
over 18
overcome 73
overwhelm 98
owe 4, 32
owing 85
own 19
ownership 77

own up to 81

page 35
pain 67
painful 75, 93
paint 72
painter 56
painting 42, 72, 98
pair 81
palace 47, 50
palate 47
pant 96
paper 35, 84
pardon 77
parent 35
Parisian 69
park 100
part 11, 13, 14
part, greater 35
particular 29
particularly 43
party 14, 31, 54
pass 7
passage 42
passion 49, 55
passionate 100
pass through 38
past 37, 55
patron 45
pattern 77
pavement 83
paw 80
pay 24
peace 22
peak 85
penetrate 43
penny 92
people 13, 19, 41
perceive 24
perceptible 57
perfect 27
perfection 94
perfectly 42
perform 81, 89
performance 90
performer 33
perfume 83

perhaps 9
period 32
permanent 61, 92
person 20
personage 49
personal 49
personality 88
phenomenon 49
philosophy 88
photograph/y 59
phrase 56
physical 60
piece 74, 82
pillar 91
pitch 55
pity 71, 74, 86
place 6, 11, 20, 36, 48
placed 66
placing 59
plain 46
plan 47, 58
plane 47
plant 79
platform 93
play 13, 66, 74, 77
please 35
pleased 84
pleasure 19
pocket 76
poem 64
poet 40
poetry 64
point 9, 85
police 66
policy 25, 66
political 30
politics 25
ponder 44
poor 25
popular 95
population 62
port 57
portrait 58
portray 24
position 19, 47
possess 25
possession 44, 73
possibility 80
possible 13

possibly 9
post 86
postpone 27
pour out 89
power 33
powerful 48
practical 82
practice 79
practise 57
pray 51
prayer 78
precaution 76
precede 87
preceding 54
precious 56
precisely 48, 71
precision 65
predict 60
prefer 63
première 50
preparation 79
prepare 29, 70
prepared 39
presence 23
present 29, 39, 44
present, to 15
present, to be 52
present time, at the 72
preserve 20, 33, 49
president 45
press 66, 67, 85
pressure 66
pretext 83
pretty 40
prevent 21
price 21
pride 100
primary 99
primitive 99
prince 51
princess 86
principal 45
principle 27
print 28
prison 61
private 29, 67
probable 92
probably 94
problem 18

proceed 64
proclaim 86
produce 25
product 46, 58
production 54
profession 35
professional 84
professor 44
profit 28, 83
profound 28
profoundly 94
programme 80
progress 59
prohibition 53
project 31
projection 60
prolong 97
promenade 71
promise 59
pronounce 39
proof 45, 48
proper 19
properly 71
property 71
proportion 80
proposal 61
propose 37
proposition 61
proprietor 61
proprietress 61
protect 98
proud 65
prove 46, 47, 93
provide 15
provide for 55
province 50
provoke 70
public 32, 41
publish 61
pull 20
pull away 63
pull off 20
pulp 63
punctual 72
pupil 60
pure 22
purpose 14, 40
pursue 34
push 31

put 6
put away 65
put down 54
put forward 55
put out 92
put to bed 55

qualification 31
quality 31
quantity 58
quarter 51, 57
quay 93
queen 64
question 11
quickly 26, 51
quite 4
quotation 26
quote 48

race 60, 75
racecourse 71
radius 69
rain 39
raise 25, 28, 38, 75
rampart 80
rank 55
rapid 60
rare 40
rather 19
ray 69
reach 28, 42
reaction 75
read 16
reader 70
reading 54
ready 39
real 32, 46
realise 38, 98
reality 29
really 20, 65
rear 89
re-ascend 53
reason 14, 70
recall 14, 41
recapture 82

receive 12, 99
recent 66
reception 54
recognise 17
recoil 82
recollection 49
recommend 92, 99
reconcile 38
recover 15, 85
red 28
redeem 65
reduce 53
reflect 44
reflection 72
refuse 26
regain 14
regard 13, 44, 75
regard to, with 49, 73
regiment 81
region 25
register 99
regret 52, 89
regular 78
regulate 73
rehearse 29
reign 92
reject 82
relation 28, 53
relative 35, 78
release 65
relief 71
religious 74, 80
remain 7, 27
remains 30
remark 22
remarkable 95
remember 41
remote 81
remove 54
renounce 64
repeat 29
repel 82
replace 27, 47
reply 31
report 28, 47, 52, 53
repose 47
represent 24, 42
representation 90
representative 82

reproach 59, 90
republic 79
reputation 98
request 78
require 40, 53
rescue 71
resemble 40
resent 70
resentment 65
reservation 57
reserve 57, 90
reserved 87
residence 72
resist 65
resistance 70
resolution 100
resolve 53
resort 94
resource 69
respect 44, 75
respected 77
respond 14
responsibility 63
rest 20, 47
result 13, 24, 32, 37
result in 74
resume 15
resumption 82
retail 22
retain 24, 33
retake 15
retire 48
retirement 87
retreat 87
return 10, 27, 34, 61
reunion 95
reunite 63, 76
reveal 31
revenge 75
reversal 34
review 58, 73
revolution 51
revolve 22
rich 34
rid 95
right 15, 41, 47, 76
right, be 14
right-hand 44
rightly 82

rigour 90
ring 63
ripe 19
risk 53, 61, 77
river 66, 97
road 16, 18, 23
rôle 26
roll 26
roof 89
room 15, 59, 65, 74
room, large 21
rose 84
rough 87
round 18, 78, 82
royal 90
rule 55, 73
rumour 41
run 25, 43
run into 82, 100
running 75, 94
Russian 71

sack 96
sacred 62
sacrifice 86, 98
sad 46, 93
sadness 99
safely 93
said 54
saint 26
sale 93
salon 47
saloon 47
same 4
satisfied 84
satisfy 63, 73
Saturday 98
save 49, 90
say 3
scatter 89
scene 26
scent 64
scheme 31
scholar 94
school 29
science 31
scientific 68

splinter 53, 63
spoke 69
spread 89
spring 49
Spring 54
square 11
squash 98
squeeze 85
stability 65
stage 26
stain 77
staircase 79
stairs 79
standard 65
star 39
start 55, 67
start again 71
state 14, 22, 33, 85
statement 92
station 56, 72, 86
statue 62
stay 27, 69
staying up 57
steady 83, 99
steer 34
step 28, 37, 64, 83
still 4
stitch 9
stoker 96
stone 39
stop 17
storey 55
story 32, 99
straight 77
strange 23, 53
stranger 68
stream 39
street 16
strength 11, 33
stretch 30, 46
stretch out 51
strike 30, 63
strip 88
strive 94
stroke 44
stroll 71
strong 18, 48
strongly 17
struggle 80, 97

student 60
studio 71
study 22, 47
stun 33
style 22, 62
subject 18, 40, 72
submit 72
subtle 98
succeed 37, 74
success 31, 32
succession 55
such 8
sudden 90
suddenly 53
suffer 26, 46
suffering 91
suffice 17
sufficient 91
sufficiently 8
sugar 71
suit 35
suit, legal 13
suite 13
sum 29
summarise 84
summary 87
Summer 40
summit 79
summon 48, 96
sun 18
Sunday 54
superior 33
supervise 87
supply 42
support 41, 49, 67
suppose 35
suppress 52
supreme 71
sure 7, 21
sure, to be 43
surely 93
surface 88
surprise 50, 78
surprised 67
surrender 52
surround 54
suspense 91
sustain 49
sway 58

swear 96
sweet 28
sweetness 92
swift 60
switch off 92
symbol 32
sympathy 79
system 36

table 18, 42
take 5
take away 91
talent 80
talk 64
tall 4, 17
task 66
taste 22, 23, 91
tax 67
teacher 44
teaching 92
tear 65
tear out 63
tears, in 65
telephone 82
tell 35
temper 58
temperature 96
tempt 52
tend 30, 81
tendency 75
tender 74
tenderness 76
term 40
terms 21
terrace 83
terrible 58
territory 72
test 45, 46, 80, 93
text 54
texture 91
thank 69
thanks 24, 96
that 1, 2, 5, 6
the 1
theatre 36
their 3
them 3

BOOKS FROM OLEANDER

A LIFETIME'S READING
Philip Ward

GREGUERIAS: THE WIT AND WISDOM OF
Ramón Gómez de la Serna

ROMONTSCH: LANGUAGE AND LITERATURE
D. B. Gregor

A DICTIONARY OF COMMON FALLACIES
Philip Ward

PUB GAMES OF ENGLAND
Timothy Finn

CELTIC: A COMPARATIVE STUDY
D. B. Gregor

HA'IL: OASIS CITY OF SAUDI ARABIA
Philip Ward

COASTAL FEATURES OF ENGLAND AND WALES
J. A. Steers

FRIULAN: LANGUAGE AND LITERATURE
D. B. Gregor

IMPOSTORS AND THEIR IMITATORS: NEW POEMS
Philip Ward

SWANSONGS: POEMS
Sue Lenier

ROMAGNOL: LANGUAGE AND LITERATURE
D. B. Gregor

COME WITH ME TO IRELAND
Philip Ward

THE GOLD-MINES OF MIDIAN
Richard Burton

CAMBRIDGE NEWSPAPERS AND OPINION
Michael Murphy

MEDICAL BOOK ILLUSTRATION: A SHORT HISTORY
J. L. Thornton & C. Reeves

MONUMENTS OF SOUTH ARABIA
Brian Doe